The Fall Of Babylon

Unlocking The End Times

Bernard Shoesmith

Published by: ADVANTAGE BOOKS™
www.advbookstore.com

Unless otherwise indicated, Bible quotations are taken from
The American Standard Version of the Bible. Copyright 1901
by Thomas Nelson & Sons.

Library of Congress Control Number: 2010931226

First Printing: August 2010
10 11 12 13 14 15 16   10 9 8 7 6 5 4 3 2 1
Printed in the United States of America

Caution

This study may challenge your views on prophecy. It is not meant to cause controversy, but to provide you with an opportunity to reflect on God's Word. It is written from an engineer's point of view, seeking to show how various end time events fit together logically and systematically. It is an attempt to show the harmony of the prophecies. There is no doubt that this study contains mistaken human thoughts. We are called to be ever vigilant and observant of a changing world. We enthusiastically await the return of our Lord. Let us join together in the study of the end times with an open mind as we see the prophecies being fulfilled.

God's Word Endures Forever

The Fall Of Babylon

Introduction

During the Gulf War, I happened to read in my private devotions the passage in Isaiah that tells of the fall of Babylon. I noticed how many of the verses, which were written thousands of years ago, were descriptive of reports in the newspaper. This sparked an interest in studying all the biblical passages that deal with Babylon and its destruction. Historical records reveal the destruction of Babylon has never happened as described in the Bible. Surprising also, within the context of Babylonian destruction, the Bible consistently describes Israel. God has placed these passages on Israel to tell us they are important within the fall of Babylon. Each verse God has given reveals details involved in the fall and must be included in the study. The various prophecies from the different prophets are in harmony. The Scriptures refer to the fall as a single event. The Scriptures are detailed in giving a literal description of its fall.

This study is not written to explain each detail, but to give a general overview of what the Scriptures say about Babylon's destruction. The Scriptures refer to the harlot Babylon as a mystery. This mystery will be solved with its destruction. The Scriptures are clear that it will be announced to the whole world. The final destruction of Babylon will not happen with

Christ's return, because the earth will be in darkness at the end of the tribulation, and God's witnesses will have been silenced. This setting does not fit the way the Scriptures say the fall will be announced to the whole world.

The prophecies throughout the Scriptures have literal fulfillments. We see this pattern from the prophecies that already have been completed. The prophecies, at their completion, are easily understood by ordinary people. Even though God tells of world events ahead of time, the actual processes of the completion are not readily known and many times are a mystery. God leaves no doubt that the prophecies are true and will be literally fulfilled just as He said.

We sense the end times are fast approaching. Some of these events no doubt are already in process. To past generations, the end-time events did not seem possible. We today can understand how they could be possible. Today we need to pay special attention to the prophecies and be aware of their messages, while at the same time taking notice of the news reports coming from that part of the world – the Middle East. What an exciting time to see God's hand at work. God recorded the prophecies to show His reality. He revealed the prophecies to His followers. As they take place, the faith of His followers will grow even stronger.

The 1901 American Standard Version of the Bible is used throughout this study. This version is considered to be one of the versions that translated the Scriptures as closely as possible, word for word, from the original language to English. I have discovered some of the other, more readable translations have taken what they felt the Scriptures were saying and transferred it to modern day language. When it comes to prophecies, many of the events in the Scriptures are unclear as to the exact details of what will happen because they are still of future events. Thus, the translators sometimes are giving us their interpretation of these verses rather than translating the verses from one language to another. This can lead to possible misunderstandings of events that are still in the future.

Table of Contents

The Fall Of Babylon

Chapter One

The Fall of Babylon is Still a Future Event

The fall of Babylon was still a future event when John wrote the book of Revelation and the prophecies recorded therein do not describe any historical events that have happened since then. With the fall of Babylon, all the prophecies about it will have been completed.

> *Isaiah 13:19-20 "And Babylon, the glory of kingdoms, the beauty of the Chaldeans' pride, shall be as when God overthrew Sodom and Gomorrah. It shall never be inhabited neither shall it be dwelt in from generation to generation: neither shall the Arabian pitch tent there; neither shall shepherds make their flocks to lie down there."*

Comment: The fall of Babylon has to be a future event because when it falls it will be completely destroyed and laid desolate, never to be inhabited again. It is not destroyed or desolate today, and people are still living there.

> *Jeremiah 50:39-40 "Therefore the wild beasts of the desert with the wolves shall dwell there, and the ostriches shall dwell therein: and it shall be no more inhabited forever; neither shall it be dwelt in from generation to generation. As when God overthrew <u>Sodom and Gomorrah</u> and the neighbor cities thereof, saith Jehovah, so shall no man dwell there, neither shall any son of <u>man sojourn therein</u>."*

Comment: There is still a town of Babylon in Iraq. Unlike Sodom and Gomorrah, which were completely destroyed and now no longer exist, Babylon remains a city in Iraq.

> *Jeremiah 51:26 "And they shall not take of thee a stone for a corner, nor a <u>stone for foundations</u>; but thou shalt be desolate forever, saith Jehovah."*

Comment: Further evidence that Babylon has not been laid completely desolate is the fact that the late Saddam Hussein was in the process of restoring the city. Saddam reused the original bricks of the ancient city and mixed them with new bricks in an attempt to restore the city to its original condition. The new bricks have his name inscribed on them.

Jeremiah 51:43-44 "Her cities are become a desolation, a dry land, and a desert, a land wherein no man dwelleth, <u>neither doth any son of man pass thereby</u>. And I will execute Judgment upon Bel in Babylon, and I will bring forth out of his mouth that which he hath swallowed up; and the nations shall not flow any more unto him: yea, the wall of Babylon shall fall."

Comment: People are still visiting the ancient ruins of Babylon. The nations of the world are still making deals with that area of the world. Commerce still takes place, people still travel through, and people still live there.

Jeremiah 51:62 "and say, O Jehovah, thou has spoken concerning this place, to cut it off, that none shall dwell therein, neither man nor beast, but that it shall be <u>desolate forever</u>."

Comment: Babylon is not desolate. "Forever" has not yet begun.

Jeremiah 51:63-64 "And it shall be, when thou hast made an end of reading this book, that thou shalt bind a <u>stone</u> to it, and cast it into the midst of the Euphrates: and thou shalt say, Thus shall Babylon <u>sink</u>, and shall not rise again because of the evil that I will bring upon her; and they shall be weary. Thus far are the words of Jeremiah."

Comment: The same illustration of the fall of Babylon is used in both Jeremiah and Revelation. The city of Babylon will disappear like a sinking stone, never to be found again.

> ***Revelation 18:21 "And a strong angel took up a <u>stone</u> as it were a great millstone and cast it into the sea, saying, thus with a mighty fall shall Babylon, the great city, be cast down, and shall be <u>found no more</u> at all."***

Comment: Babylon can still be found today, so it has not been cast down forever.

> ***Revelation 17:6 "And I saw the woman drunken with the blood of the saints, and with the blood of the <u>martyrs of Jesus</u>. And when I saw her, I wondered with great wonder."***

Comment: There were no martyrs of Jesus until after His return to heaven. Since the time of Jesus, history does not record a fall. Thus it is still a future event.

<u>Summary: The Fall of Babylon is Still a Future Event</u>

There are many verses that talk of the fall of Babylon. It is an event that God wants the world to know. From the previous verses, it is logical to conclude that the prophecies have not been literally fulfilled. The final destruction is still a future event. Where we as individuals place the fall of Babylon in time will influence our view of end-time events.

Announcing the Fall of Babylon:
When, to Whom, and by Whom

Isaiah 21:9 "and, behold, here cometh a troop of men, horsemen in pairs. And he answered and said, <u>Fallen, fallen is Babylon</u>; and all the graven images of her gods are broken unto the ground."

Jeremiah 51:8 "Babylon is suddenly <u>fallen</u> and destroyed: wail for her; take balm for her pain, if so she may be healed."

Revelation 14:8 "And another, a second angel, followed, saying, <u>Fallen, fallen</u> is Babylon the great, that hath made all the nations to drink of the wine of the wrath of her fornication."

Revelation 18:2 "And he cried with a mighty voice, saying, <u>Fallen, fallen</u> is Babylon the great, and is become a habitation of demons, and a hold of every unclean spirit, and a hold of every unclean and hateful bird."

Comment: The announcement of Babylon's fall is in the past tense, not as an announcement of future destruction. After the fall it will no longer be a mystery, but clearly known. Many details are given about the fall, but the sudden end will fit together all the pieces. God's prophetic message will be realized and clearly understood. God uses the words "Fallen, fallen" thus possibly telling us that Babylon falls twice.

Jeremiah 50:2 "Declare ye among the nations and publish, and set up a standard; <u>publish</u>, <u>and conceal not</u>: say, Babylon is taken, Bel is put to shame, Merodach is dismayed; her images are put to shame, her idols are dismayed."

Comment: God does not want the message of the fall of Babylon to be concealed.

Jeremiah 50:28 "<u>The voice of them that flee and escape</u> out of the land of Babylon, to declare in Zion the vengeance of Jehovah our God, the vengeance of His temple."

Comment: Eyewitnesses flee to Zion and testify of God's vengeance against Babylon.

Jeremiah 51:48 "Then the <u>heavens and the earth</u>, and all that is therein, shall sing for joy over Babylon; for the destroyers shall come unto her from the north, saith Jehovah."

Comment: Not only is the fall of Babylon known on the earth, but also in the heavens.

Isaiah 48:20 "Go ye forth from Babylon, flee ye from the Chaldeans; with a voice of singing declare ye, tell this, utter it even to the <u>end of the earth</u>: say ye, Jehovah hath <u>redeemed his servant Jacob</u>."

Comment: As part of the announcement, through the fall of Babylon God redeems Israel and it will be told to the ends of the earth.

Revelation 18:20 "Rejoice over her, thou heaven, and ye saints, and ye apostles, and ye prophets; for God hath judged your judgment on her."

Comment: The fall causes rejoicing by all of God's people who have experienced her wickedness.

Revelation 19:1-4 "After these things I heard as it were a great voice of a great multitude in heaven saying, Hallelujah; Salvation, and glory, and power, belong to our God: for true and righteous are his judgments; for he hath judged the great harlot, her that corrupted the earth with her fornication, and he hath avenged the blood of his servants at her hand. And a second time they say, Hallelujah. And her smoke goeth up forever and ever. And the four and twenty elders and the four living creatures fell down and worshipped God that sitteth on the throne, saying, Amen; Hallelujah."

Comment: When the fall of Babylon takes place, those on God's side in heaven will rejoice and praise God. God's judgments are righteous. The harlot Babylon has corrupted the earth, causing the blood of God's servants to be spilled.

Revelation 18:9 "And the kings of the earth, who committed fornication and lived wantonly with her, shall weep and wail over her, when they look upon the smoke of her burning."

Comment: The kings of the earth realize that their opportunity to receive benefits from their relationship with Babylon is gone. They are in shock and mourning.

Revelation 18:11 "And the <u>merchants of the earth</u> weep and mourn over her, for no man buyeth their merchandise any more."

Comment: The merchants weep because the fall of Babylon causes the loss of their business.

<u>Summary: Announcing the Fall of Babylon: When, to Whom, and by Whom</u>

The fall is known and announced after the event happens. The announcement results in different reactions. The world is in shock and mourning because they realize their relationship with Babylon no longer exists. She will no longer be able to meet their needs.

God's people, both the deceased and the living, will be rejoicing in heaven and on earth. On earth the message will be clearly announced by God's followers telling how God has delivered Israel; how God is judging the evil caused by Babylon and the details of the prophetic message from the prophets. The prophets will experience what they had written about years ago. The saints martyred by the wickedness of Babylon's influence know that God has finally avenged Babylon for her deeds. The world is in shock as they see the total destruction and the effects that it has on them.

****

The Fall of Babylon -Those Involved in the Destruction

Isaiah 13:3-5 "I have commanded my consecrated ones, yea, I have called my mighty men for mine anger, even my proudly exulting ones. The noise of a multitude in the mountains, as of a great people! the noise of a tumult of the <u>kingdoms of the nations</u> gathered together! Jehovah of hosts is mustering the host for the battle. They come from a far country, from the <u>uttermost part of heaven</u>, even Jehovah, and the <u>weapons of his</u> <u>indignation</u>, to destroy the whole land."

Comment: Those involved in the fall of Babylon include the kingdoms of the nations gathered by God. The spirit world, which is unseen by humans, will also be involved. God also uses His weapons such as wind, sandstorms, and rain.

Isaiah 13:17-18 "Behold I will stir up the <u>Medes</u> against them, who shall <u>not regard silver, and as</u> <u>for gold</u>, they shall not delight in it. And their bows shall dash the young men in pieces; and they shall have no pity on the fruit of the womb; their eye shall not spare children."

Comment: Today the Kurdish people live where the Medes were. They are known for their bloody revenge. They will not be bought off.

Isaiah 21:2 "A grievous vision is declared unto me; the treacherous man dealeth treacherously, *and the destroyer destroyeth. Go up, <u>O Elam</u>; besiege, <u>O Media</u>; all the sighing thereof have I made to cease."*

Comment: Not only are the Medes or Kurds involved, but also Elam, a people group currently represented in western Iran.

Isaiah 48:14 "Assemble yourselves, all ye, and hear; who among them hath declared these things? He <u>whom Jehovah loveth</u> shall perform his pleasure on Babylon, and his arm shall be on the Chaldeans."

Comment: "He whom Jehovah loveth" refers to Israel. Therefore, Israel will also be involved.

Jeremiah 50:9-10 "For, lo, I will stir up and cause to come up against Babylon a company of <u>great nations from the north country</u>; and they shall set themselves in array against her; from thence she shall be taken: their arrows shall be as of an expert mighty man; <u>none shall return in vain</u>. And <u>Chaldea</u> shall be a prey: all that prey upon her shall be satisfied, saith Jehovah."

Comment: Great nations (plural) that are north of Babylon will be involved. Their battle will be a total success and none will come back defeated. Chaldea originally referred to a small territory in southern Babylonia at the head of the Persian Gulf. At the present time it is represented by modern day Kuwait.

Jeremiah 50:25-27 "Jehovah hath opened his armory, and hath brought forth the weapons of his indignation; for the Lord, Jehovah of hosts, hath a work to do in the land of the Chaldeans. Come against her from the <u>utmost border</u>; open her storehouses; . . . let them go down to the slaughter: woe unto them! for their day is come, the time of their visitation. "

Comment: In the Gulf War, the countries represented came from all over the earth. Soldiers from each continent came to help.

Jeremiah 50:41 "Behold, a people cometh from the north; and a <u>great nation and many kings</u> shall be stirred up from the <u>uttermost parts of the earth</u>. "

Comment: If the fall of Babylon is now in progress, we know that, "A people cometh from the north" refers to the Kurds. "A great nation" refers to the United States. "Uttermost parts" refers to the coalition of nations formed during the Gulf War.

Jeremiah 51:1-2 "Thus saith Jehovah: behold, I will raise up against Babylon, and against them that dwell in Leb-kamai, a destroying wind. And I will send unto Babylon <u>strangers</u>, that shall winnow her; and they shall empty her land: for in the <u>day of trouble</u> they shall be <u>against her</u> round about. "

Comment: The "strangers" that will winnow Babylon refer to people not from Babylon (terrorists). During the days of her troubles they cause destruction.

> *Revelation 17:16-17 "And the <u>ten horns</u> which thou sawest, and the beast, these shall hate the harlot, and shall make her <u>desolate and naked</u>, and shall eat her flesh, and shall burn her utterly <u>with fire</u>. For God did put in their hearts to do his mind, and to come to one mind, and to give their kingdom unto the beast, until the words of God should be accomplished."*
>
> *Isaiah 47:3 " Thy <u>nakedness shall be uncovered</u>, yea, thy shame shall be seen: <u>I</u> will take vengeance, and will spare no man."*
>
> *Isaiah 47:14 "Behold, they shall be as stubble; the <u>fire shall burn them</u>; they shall not deliver themselves from the power of the flame: it shall not be a coal to warm at, nor a fire to sit before."*

Comment: The fall of Babylon will reveal the ten horns of the beast. The ten horns have control over that part of the world. They allow the entire world to come together to bring about the destruction.

<u>Summary: Those Involved in Destruction</u>

The Scriptures tell us that this event will involve nations from around the globe. They mention that a people group; a great nation and many kings from around the world will send their soldiers. Also involved is the spirit world, even God himself. It is not just a localized event in that part of the world; it affects the whole world. Each group has a part in the total destruction of Babylon.

****

The Fall of Babylon - Time Involved

Jeremiah 50:9 "For, lo, I will stir up and cause to come up against Babylon <u>a company of</u> <u>great</u> <u>nations</u> from the north country; and they shall set themselves in array against her; from thence she shall be taken: their arrows shall be as of an expert mighty man; none shall return in vain."

Comment: The assembling of the armies of the world against Babylon takes time to prepare and to coordinate the various nations' armies.

Isaiah 47:11 "Therefore shall evil come upon thee; thou shalt not know the dawning thereof: and mischief shall fall upon thee; thou shalt not be able to put it away: and desolation shall come upon thee <u>suddenly, which thou knowest not.</u>"

Comment: The destruction will happen suddenly and will be a surprise that Babylon had not anticipated.

Jeremiah 51:45-47 "<u>My people</u>, go ye out of the midst of her, and save yourselves every man from *the fierce anger of Jehovah. And let not your heart faint, neither fear ye for the tidings that shall be heard in the land; for <u>tidings shall come one year</u>, and after that in <u>another year</u> shall come tidings, and violence in the land, ruler against ruler. Therefore, behold, the days come, that I will execute judgment upon the graven images of Babylon; and her whole land shall be confounded; and all her slain shall fall in the midst of her."*

Comment: There are several years involved. This involves the removal of God's people from Babylon. There will be violence in the land with ruler against ruler. This situation not only affects Babylon, but also in some way causes fear in Israel.

Revelation 18:8 "Therefore in <u>one day shall her plagues come</u>, death, and mourning, and famine; and she shall be utterly burned with fire; for strong is the Lord God who judged her."

Comment: A decision enacted on a certain date can bring these plagues into place in one day, such as an embargo.

Isaiah 47:9 "but these two things shall come to thee in a <u>moment in one day</u>, the loss of children, and widowhood; in their full measure shall they come upon thee, in the multitude of thy sorceries, and the great abundance of thine enchantments."

Comment: Loss of husband or children causes mourning at the moment it happens.

> *Revelation 18:18-19 "and cried out as they looked upon the smoke of her burning, saying, What city is like the great city? And they cast dust on their heads, and cried, weeping and mourning, saying, Woe, woe, the great city, wherein all that had their ships in the sea were made rich by reason of her costliness! for in <u>one hour</u> is she made desolate."*

Comment: Babylon is burned up with fire. In one hour all of the riches and physical development go up in smoke. The fire is the final step, with only smoke lingering.

Summary: Time Involved

As we look at the time involved, we note that though it refers to several years, yet suddenly, one day her plagues come, and in one hour there will be total destruction.

It would seem these are contradictory statements but they will not be. They are just different ways of looking at the destruction process and its various events. Babylon is referred to as mystery Babylon. In the end the mystery will be known and solved. All of the prophets' verses will have their fulfillment. Presently we do not know the exact sequence.

****

The Fall of Babylon - The Significance of World Events

> *Jeremiah 50:14-16 "Set yourselves in array against Babylon round about, all ye that bend the bow; shoot at her, <u>spare no arrows</u>: for she hath sinned against Jehovah. Shout against her round about: she hath submitted herself; her bulwarks are fallen, her walls are thrown down; for it is the vengeance of Jehovah: take vengeance upon her; as she hath done, do unto her. Cut off the sower from Babylon, and him that handleth the sickle in the time of harvest: for fear of the oppressing sword they shall turn every one to his people, and <u>they shall flee every one to his own land.</u>*

Comment: Hundreds of missiles were fired every day during the Gulf War. Certainly no missiles were spared as each plane returned for more. The foreigners who were working in Iraq at the time were scattered trying to get home to their own countries.

> *Jeremiah 51:1-4 "Thus saith Jehovah: Behold, I will raise up against Babylon, and against them that dwell in Leb-kamai, a destroying wind. And I will <u>send unto Babylon strangers</u>, that shall winnow her; and they shall <u>empty her land</u>: for in the day of trouble they shall be against her round about. Against him that bendeth let the archer bend his bow, and against him that lifteth himself up in his coat of mail: and spare ye not her young men; destroy ye utterly all her host.*

And they shall fall down slain in the land of the Chaldeans, and thrust through in her streets."

Comment: This could be referring to the terrorists who are coming from other countries to defeat the United States and keep Iraq from becoming a democratic country.

Jeremiah 51:8-9 "Babylon is <u>suddenly fallen</u> and destroyed: wail for her; take balm for her pain, if so be she may be healed. We would have healed Babylon, but she <u>is not</u> <u>healed</u>: forsake her, and let us go every one into his own country; for her judgment reacheth unto heaven, and is lifted up even to the skies."

Comment: When the US and the coalition forces entered Iraq, Iraq was easily defeated and now it is in the process of being rebuilt. Currently there is little progress in rebuilding Iraq as a democratic nation. American troops are not yet able to return to the States. In the end the nations give up and return to their own countries. The fall of Babylon is an event that will take time to complete. In the end Iraq will not be rebuilt as a nation.

Jeremiah 51:30-32 "The mighty men of Babylon have forborne to fight, they <u>remain in their</u> <u>strongholds</u>; their might hath failed; they are become as women: her dwelling-places are set on fire; her bars are broken. One post shall run to meet another, and one messenger to meet another, to show the king of Babylon that his city is taken on every quarter: and the <u>passages are</u>

> *seized, and the reeds they have burned with fire, and the men of war are affrighted."*

Comment: During the Gulf War, the Iraqi soldiers stayed in their bunkers and were bombed daily. They tried to protect the bridges from being bombed by setting fires that made a lot of smoke, so the airplanes could not see where the bridges were.

> *Isaiah 13:10 "For the stars of heaven and the constellations thereof shall not give their light; the sun shall be darkened in its going forth, and the moon shall not cause its light to shine."*

Comment: This passage can be illustrated by the burning of the oil wells in Kuwait. The people there needed their headlights on at noon to see to drive.

> *Isaiah 13:14-16 "And it shall come to pass, that as the chased roe, and as sheep that no man gathereth, they shall turn every man to his own people, and shall flee every man to his own land. Every one that is found shall be thrust through; and every one that is taken shall fall by the sword. Their infants also shall be dashed in pieces before their eyes; their houses shall be rifled, and their wives ravished."*

Comment: During the Gulf War, there were several hundred thousand people who were massed on the Jordanian border trying to get out of the country to return to their home country. Some were running from one house to another hiding, trying not to get caught. Iraq reinstated the law that the foreigners and those harboring them should be killed. In Kuwait some of the children caught at the mall were taken home and shot in front of their families.

Isaiah 14:1-2 "For Jehovah will have compassion on Jacob, and will yet choose Israel, and set them in their own land: and the sojourner shall join himself with them, and they shall cleave to the house of Jacob. And the peoples shall take them, and bring them to their place; and the house of Israel shall possess them in the land of Jehovah for <u>servants and for handmaids</u>: and they shall take them captive whose captives they were; and they shall rule over their oppressors.

Comment: During the Gulf War, when Israel closed its borders it caused a problem, as the Palestine people were unable to go to work in the homes of Israelis. These verses are not yet completely fulfilled, but illustrate how the Palestinians are workers in the Israeli homes.

Isaiah 14:16-21 "They that see thee shall gaze at thee, they shall consider thee, saying, Is this the man that <u>made the earth to tremble</u>, that did shake kingdoms; that made the world as a wilderness, and overthrew the cities thereof; that let not loose his prisoners to their home? All the kings of the nations, all of them, sleep in glory, every one in his own house. But thou art cast forth away <u>from thy sepulcher</u> like an *__abominable branch__, clothed with the slain, that are thrust through with the sword, that go down to the stones of the pit; as a deal body trodden under foot. Thou shalt not be joined with them in burial, because thou hast __destroyed thy land__, thou hast __slain thy people__; the seed of evildoers shall not be named forever. Prepare ye __slaughter for his children__ for the iniquity of their fathers, that they rise not up, and possess the earth, and fill the face of the world with cities."*

Comment: During the Gulf War, the nations were guarding the oil wells and other interests because of the threats Saddam was making. This was done because they were afraid of what he might do. Saddam was executed; he did not receive the burial of a king. However, US President Gerald Ford's funeral happened at about the same time and he received the burial of a king. When they pulled down Saddam's statue, they dragged it through the streets while hitting its head with their shoes. It should be noted that before the king of Babylon can be cast out of his sepulcher he must have been buried first. Saddam was executed because he gassed the Kurds. Saddam's sons were just as cruel as he was and were wanted dead or alive. They were gunned down.

Isaiah 21:9 "and, behold, here cometh a troop of men __horsemen in pairs__. And he answered and said, Fallen, fallen is Babylon; and all the graven images of her gods are broken unto the ground."

Comment: It is interesting to note the fighter jets going to bomb Iraq were flown by a pilot and a co-pilot.

Summary: World Events

Many aspects of the prophecies concerning the fall of Babylon can be illustrated by recent news reports. Even though we do not know how the war in Iraq will end, we need to pay special attention to the prophecies. It is possible that we are now in the process of experiencing the fulfillment of prophecies written over two thousand years ago. There are many different ways the prophetic verses of Babylon can be interpreted. All possibilities should be considered. At the same time, we should reject world events where the Scriptures reveal that they do not fit. Today there are more world events in Iraq illustrated in the Scriptures than when Babylon fell the first time.

****

The Fall Of Babylon

Chapter Two

Israel Within The Context Of The Fall Of Babylon

Israel Before the Fall

> *Jeremiah: 50:6-8 "My people have been lost sheep: <u>their shepherds have caused them to go astray</u>; they have turned them away on the mountains; they have gone from mountain to hill; they have forgotten their resting-place. All that found them have devoured them; and their adversaries said, We are not guilty, because they have sinned against Jehovah, the habitation of righteousness, even Jehovah, the hope of their fathers. <u>Flee out of the midst of Babylon</u>, and go forth out of the land of the Chaldeans, and be as the he-goats before the flocks."*

Comment: This is the result of following human leadership, instead of receiving Christ as their Messiah. During the Gulf War, there were no people from Israel listed in the newspapers trying to get out of Iraq. The Israeli people already had realized that Iraq was not their friend.

Jeremiah 50:17 "<u>Israel is a hunted sheep</u>; the lions have driven him away: first, the king of Assyria devoured him; and now at last Nebuchadnezzar king of Babylon hath broken his bones."

Comment: Evil nations have never loved God's chosen people.

Jeremiah 51:5-6 "For Israel is not <u>forsaken,</u> nor Judah, of his God, of Jehovah of hosts; though their land is <u>full of guilt</u> against the Holy One of Israel. <u>Flee out of the midst of Babylon</u>, and save every man his life; be not cut off in her iniquity: for it is the time of Jehovah's vengeance; he will render unto her a recompense."

Comment: Israel's land is full of guilt against God but God has not forsaken them. The people of Israel are no longer living in Iraq.

Jeremiah 50:33 "Thus saith Jehovah of hosts: The children of Israel and the children of Judah are oppressed together; and all that took them <u>captive hold them fast; they refuse to let them go</u>."

Comment: Two major countries of the world (Germany and Russia) have had control over the Jews and have oppressed them, and have not allowed them to move somewhere else.

> *Isaiah 48:15-19 "I, even I, have spoken; yea, I have called him; I have brought him, and he shall make his way prosperous. Come ye near unto me, hear ye this; from the beginning I have not spoken in secret; from the time that it was, there am I: and now the Lord Jehovah hath sent me, and his Spirit. Thus saith Jehovah, they Redeemer, the Holy One of Israel: I am Jehovah thy God, who teacheth thee to profit, who leadeth thee by the way that thou shouldest go. Oh that thou hadst hearkened to my commandments! then had thy peace been as a river, and thy righteousness as the waves of the sea: thy seed also had been as the sand, and the offspring of thy bowels like the grains thereof: his name would not be cut off nor destroyed from before me."*

Comment: God is the one who has taught Israel to profit. If Israel had obeyed God's commands, they would have lived in peace. Their righteousness would have honored God and they would have multiplied as a nation.

> *Jeremiah 51:45-56 "My people, go ye out of the midst of her, and save yourselves every man from the fierce anger of Jehovah. And let not your heart faint, neither fear ye for the tidings that shall be heard in the land; for tidings shall come one year, and after that in another year shall*

come tidings, and violence in the land, ruler against ruler."

Comment: Their hearts will be faint and living in fear at several times in different years as they see the news of how they are being threatened or attacked.

Isaiah 48:1-2 "Hear ye this, O house of Jacob, who are called by the name of Israel, and are come forth out of the waters of Judah; who swear by the name of Jehovah, and make mention of the God of Israel, but not in <u>truth, nor in righteousness</u> (for they call themselves of the holy city, and stay themselves upon the God of Israel; Jehovah of hosts ins his name).

Comment: Even though Israel claims to have the Holy City of God and to be His chosen people, they do it not in truth or righteousness. They have rejected God's Son, Jesus, and His message to them as the Messiah.

Isaiah 48:8-10 "Yea, thou heardest not; yea, thou knewest not; yea, from of old thine ear was not opened: for I knew that thou didst deal very treacherously, and was called a transgressor from the womb. For my <u>name's sake</u> will I defer mine anger, and for my praise will I refrain for thee, that I cut thee not off. Behold, I have refined thee, but not as silver; I have chosen thee in the <u>furnace of affliction.</u>"

Comment: For His name's sake, God will not completely destroy Israel even though they reject Him. The furnace of affliction is a good term for the gas chambers and the burning of the Jews during World War II.

Summary: Israel before the Fall

Within the context of the fall of Babylon, we continually find mention of the country of Israel. Before the fall, God has not forgotten Israel, even though they are experiencing the results of not following God.

****

Israel during the Fall

> *Jeremiah 50:4-5 "In those days, and in that time, saith Jehovah, the children of Israel shall come, they and the children of Judah together; they shall go on their way weeping, and shall seek Jehovah their God. They shall inquire concerning Zion with their faces thitherward, saying, Come ye, and join yourselves to Jehovah in an everlasting covenant that shall not be forgotten."*

Comment: The people of Israel will realize their state of hopelessness and demonstrate in the streets seeking for God's help. They promise to follow God if He will deliver them. The verse before these refers to the coming war, which causes people to flee. The problem of Babylon causes Israel to go in the streets asking for God's help.

Jeremiah 50:44 "Behold, the enemy shall come up like a lion from the pride of the Jordan <u>against the strong habitation</u>: for I will suddenly make them run away from it; and whoso is chosen, him will I appoint over it: for who is like me? and who will appoint me a time? and who is the shepherd that can stand before me?"

Comment: In the context of the destruction of Babylon, Israel will be attacked and dragged into the battle. Still, God will not allow others to take control of Israel.

Jeremiah 51:19 "The portion of Jacob is not like these; for he is the former of all things; and Israel is the tribe of his <u>inheritance</u>: Jehovah of hosts is his name."

Comment: God favors Israel and they will not be destroyed like Babylon.

Jeremiah 51: 20-24 "<u>Thou art my battle-axe and weapons of war</u>: and with thee will I break in pieces the nations; and with thee will <u>I destroy kingdoms</u>; and with thee will I break in pieces the horse and his rider; and with thee will I break in pieces the chariot and him that rideth therein; and with thee will I break in pieces <u>man</u> and <u>woman</u>; and with thee will I break in pieces the old man and <u>the youth</u>; and with thee will I break in pieces the young man and <u>the virgin</u>; and with thee will I break in pieces <u>the shepherd</u> and his flock; and with thee will I break in pieces <u>the husbandman</u>

and his yoke **of oxen;** *and with thee will I break in pieces* <u>*governors and deputies.*</u> **"**

Comment: God uses Israel as His battle-axe. As the nations come against Israel, they will be defeated. The destruction affects all levels of society.

Isaiah 14:1 "For Jehovah will have compassion on Jacob, and will yet choose Israel, and <u>set them in their own land:</u> and the sojourner shall join himself with them, and they shall cleave to the house of Jacob."

Comment: God will have compassion on Israel and they will once again get their land back.

<u>Summary: Israel during the Fall</u>

Israel realizes their hopelessness and the threat against their nation. They march in the streets, asking for God's help. They promise to keep the everlasting covenant with God. God will have compassion on Israel and place them in their own land. He will use Israel as His battle-axe to cause in one way or another the destruction of Babylon.

****

Israel after the Fall

Jeremiah 50:19-20 "And I will bring <u>Israel again to his pasture,</u> and he shall feed on <u>Carmel and Bashan,</u> and his soul shall be satisfied upon *the hills of **Ephraim** and in **Gilead**. In those days, and in that time, saith Jehovah, the **iniquity of Israel** shall be sought for, and there shall be none; and the sins of Judah, and they shall not be found: for I will pardon them whom I leave as a remnant."*

Comment: Israel will have control over Carmel, or northern Israel, which they currently control, Bashan, (the Golan Heights), Gilead (east of the Jordan River, located in Jordan today), and Ephraim (the West Bank). Some nations will seek to make Israel return the land that they capture but God will allow them to keep it in their possession because the nations realize Israel has tried to live in peace with their neighbors who have insisted they should be wiped off the face of the earth.

*Jeremiah 50:34 "Their Redeemer is strong; Jehovah of hosts is his name: he will thoroughly plead their cause, that he may give **rest to the earth**, and disquiet the inhabitants of Babylon."*

Comment: Because of the peace with Israel, the earth is at rest but the inhabitants on Babylon's side are left fearful. The forces against Israel have been defeated.

*Isaiah 14:1-3 "For Jehovah will have compassion on Jacob, and will yet choose Israel, and set them in their **own land:** and the sojourner shall join himself with them, and they shall cleave to the house of Jacob. And the peoples shall take them, and bring them to their* *place; and the house of Israel shall possess them in the land of Jehovah <u>for servants</u> <u>and for handmaids</u>: and they shall take them captive whose captives they were; and they shall rule over their oppressors. And it shall come to pass in the day that Jehovah shall give thee <u>rest from thy sorrow</u>, and from thy trouble, and from the hard service wherein thou wast made to serve."*

Comment: Israel will be at peace in their land. The Arabs will become servants and handmaids in the Israeli homes. Israel will have control over the Arabs living there. Israel will be given rest from the sorrow they were forced to endure.

Summary: Israel after the Fall

In the context of the fall of Babylon, Israel will be given all their land. They will have rest from their sorrows. They will rule over those who have oppressed them. The earth will be given rest from the Middle East problem. God will bring about a major power shift that allows Israel to live in peace. It sounds to me like the perfect opportunity to rebuild the temple.

****

The Fall Of Babylon

Chapter Three

Characteristics of Babylon at the Fall

Isaiah 14:5-6 "Jehovah hath broken the staff of the wicked, the scepter of the rulers; that smote the peoples in <u>wrath</u> with a <u>continual stroke</u>, that ruled the nations in anger, with a persecution that none restrained."

Comment: Their rulers continually smote people with their wickedness. No one was able to stop or control the persecution. This caused anger among the nations.

Isaiah 47:8-10 "Now therefore hear this, thou that art given to pleasures, that sittest securely, that sayest in thy heart, <u>I am, and there is none else besides me</u>; I shall not sit as a widow, neither shall I know the loss of children: but these two things shall come to thee in a moment in one day, the loss of children: but these two things shall come to thee in a moment in one day, the loss of children, and widowhood; in their full measure shall they come upon thee, in the multitude of <u>thy sorceries</u>, and the great *abundance of thine <u>enchantments</u>. For thou hast <u>trusted in thy wickedness</u>; thou hast said, <u>None seeth me</u>; thy wisdom and thy knowledge, it hath perverted thee, and thou hast said in thy heart, I am, and there is none else besides me."*

Comment: The rulers of Babylon demand things be done their way. They are led by evil spirits. They trust in their wickedness, done in such a way that no one knows it, a perfect description of terrorism. They get their way by doing evil things.

Isaiah 47:12-13 "Stand now with thine enchantments, and with the multitude of thy sorceries, wherein thou has labored from thy youth; if so thou shalt be able to profit, if so be thou mayest prevail. Thou are wearied in the multitude of thy counsels: let now the astrologers, the <u>star-gazers</u>, the <u>monthly prognosticators</u>, stand up, and <u>save thee</u> from the things that shall come upon thee."

Comment: Their astrologers, the prognosticators and their multitude of counselors are unable to show them how to save themselves.

Jeremiah 50:11-13 "Because ye are glad, because ye rejoice, O ye that <u>plunder my heritage</u>, because ye are wanton as a heifer that treadeth out the grain, and neigh as strong horses; your mother shall be utterly put to shame; she that bare you shall be confounded:

behold, she shall be the hindermost of the nations, a wilderness, a dry land, and a desert. Because of the <u>wrath of Jehovah</u> she shall not be inhabited, but she shall be wholly desolate: every one that goeth by Babylon shall be astonished, and hiss at all her plagues."

Comment: God's wrath comes because they plunder His heritage (Israel).

Jeremiah 50:14-16 "Set yourselves in array against <u>Babylon round about</u>, all ye that bend the bow; shoot at her, spare no arrows: for she hath sinned against Jehovah. Shout against her round about: she hath submitted herself; her bulwarks are fallen, her walls are thrown down; for it is the vengeance of Jehovah: take vengeance upon her; as she hath done, do unto her. Cut off the sower from Babylon, and him that handleth the sickle in the time of harvest: for fear of the oppressing sword they shall turn every one to his people, and they shall <u>flee</u> every one to his <u>own land</u>."

Comment: Babylon is surrounded on all sides. She will receive the same vengeance she has shown towards others. Because of the fear of the coming war, the foreign workers were fleeing, trying to get out and return to their homelands.

Jeremiah 51:7 "Babylon hath been a golden cup in Jehovah's hand, that made all the earth

*drunken: the nations have drunk of her wine;
therefore the <u>nations are mad</u>."*

Comment: The nations have been influenced by Babylon,
and have become drunk like her. They are mad because they
follow evil instead of God's plan.

*Jeremiah 51:41-44 "How is Sheshach taken!
And the praise of the whole earth seized! How is
Babylon become a desolation among the nations!
The sea is come up upon Babylon; she is covered
with the multitude of the waves thereof. Her
cities are become a desolation, a dry land, and a
desert, <u>a land wherein no man dwelleth</u>, neither
doth <u>any son of mass pass thereby</u>. And I will
execute judgment upon Bel in Babylon, and I
will bring forth out of his mouth that which he
hath swallowed up; and the nations shall not
flow any more unto him: yea, the wall of Babylon
shall fall."*

Comment: No one will be able to live in Babylon or even
pass by because of the contamination that results from its total
destruction.

*Zechariah 5:5-11 "Then the angel that talked
with me went forth, and said unto me, Lift up
now thine eyes, and see what is this that goeth
forth. And I said, What is it? And he said, This is
the ephah that goeth forth. He said moreover,
This is their appearance in all the land (and,
behold, there was lifted up a talent of lead); and*

this is a woman sitting in the midst of the ephah. And he said, <u>This is Wickedness</u>; and he cast her down into the midst of the ephah; and he cast the weight of lead upon the mouth thereof. Then lifted I up mine eyes, and saw, and, behold, there came forth two women, and the wind was in their wings; now they had wings like the wings of a stork; and they lifted up the ephah between earth and heaven. Then said I to the angel that talked with me, Whither do these bear the ephah? And he said unto me, To build her a house in the <u>land of Shinar</u>: and when it is prepared, she shall be <u>set there in her own place.</u>"

Comment: We are told here that the harlot Babylon is wickedness. A base will be established there in Babylon to support her wickedness.

Revelation 17:3-6 "And he carried me away in the Spirit into a wilderness: and I saw a woman sitting upon a scarlet-colored beast, full of <u>names of blasphemy, having seven heads and ten horns</u>. And the woman was arrayed in purple and scarlet, and decked with gold and precious stone and pearls, having in her hand a <u>golden cup full of abominations</u>, even the unclean things of her fornication, and upon her forehead a name written, MYSTERY, BABYLON THE GREAT, THE MOTHER OF THE HARLOTS AND OF THE ABOMINATINS OF THE EARTH. And I saw the woman <u>drunken with the blood of the saints</u>, and with the blood of the martyrs of

Jesus. And when I saw her, I wondered with a great wonder."

Comment: The woman depicted here is found in the wilderness and rides on the end-time beast, which has seven heads and ten horns. This beast, which was formed down through ages, represents kingdoms that blasphemed God. They blasphemed God by placing their power and their gods over God's chosen people, Israel. This beast does not yet have ten crowns, so Babylon is not riding on the eighth end-time beast, which has ten crowns on the ten horns. The woman's wine is the killing of the saints and martyrs of Jesus down through the ages. Babylon has given to the earth the abominations against God. They have chosen their power and riches over God's plan for His creation.

Revelation 18:7 "How much soever she glorified herself, and waxed wanton, so much give her of torment and mourning: for she saith in her heart, I sit a queen, and am no widow, and shall in no wise see mourning."

Comment: This is the same description as was used in **Isaiah 47:8**. Babylon was determined to have her way at all costs.

Revelation 18:11-13 "And the merchants of the earth weep and mourn over her, for no man buyeth their merchandise any more; merchandise of gold, and silver, and precious stone, and pearls, and fine linen, and purple, and silk, and scarlet; and all thyine wood, and every *vessel of ivory, and every vessel made of most precious wood, and of brass, and iron, and marble; and cinnamon, and spice, and incense, and ointment, and frankincense, and wine, and oil, and fine flour, and wheat, and cattle, and sheep; and merchandise of horses and chariots and slaves; and <u>souls of men</u>.*"

Comment: Riches from oil production were used to purchase everything they wanted; the love of money is the root of all evil. Saddam was buying souls of men when he paid money to the families of the suicide bombers. Today merchandise of all types pours into Iraq as they try to rebuild.

<u>Summary: Characteristics of Babylon</u>

Many of the characteristics of Babylon can be illustrated by Saddam's actions. He continually ruled his people in anger that no one was able to stop. He trusted in wickedness. He paid for suicide bombers to attack Israel. Even though his country was surrounded on all sides, he stood firm demanding things his way. He caused fear all over the world by his threats, causing them to respond to his actions. He even had a portrait done of himself with King Nebuchadnezzar on equal bases. Iraq today has become a center for the battles against wickedness. Today the ships of the world are carrying merchandise of all types for the rebuilding of Iraq.

****

Possibility of a Nuclear Bomb

Isaiah 13:6-8 "Wail ye; for the day of Jehovah is at hand; as destruction from the Almighty shall it come. Therefore shall all hands be feeble, and every heart of man shall melt: and they shall be dismayed; pangs and sorrows shall take hold of them; they shall be in pain as a woman in travail: they shall look in amazement one at another; their faces shall be faces of flame."

Comment: The destruction of Babylon seems to affect everyone. They see each other's faces go up in flames.

Isaiah 13:21-22 "But wild beasts of the desert shall lie there; and their houses shall be full of doleful creatures; and ostriches shall dwell there, and wild goats shall dance there. And wolves shall cry in their castles, and jackals in the pleasant palaces: and her time is near to come, and her days shall not be prolonged."

Comment: Animals will return and live there but they are not normal. Man is no longer able to live there.

Isaiah 14:23 "I will also make it a possession for the porcupine, and pools of water: and I will sweep it with the besom of destruction, saith Jehovah of hosts."

Comment: Animals and water are there, but no humans.

Jeremiah 50:32 "And the proud one shall stumble and fall, and none shall raise him up;

and I will kindle a <u>fire in his cities</u>, and it shall devour all that are round about him."

Comment: "Fire" is singular, while "cities" is plural. It could be that one fire destroys the whole area.

Jeremiah 51:20-26 "Thou art my battle-axe and weapons of war: and with thee will I break in pieces the nations; and with thee will I destroy kingdoms; and with thee will I break in pieces the horse and his rider; and with thee will I break in pieces the chariot and him that rideth therein; and with thee will I break in pieces man and woman; and with thee will I break in pieces the old man and the youth; and with thee will I break in pieces the young man and the virgin; and with thee will I break in pieces the shepherd and his flock; and with thee will I break in pieces the husbandman and his yoke of oxen; and with thee will I break in pieces governors and deputies. And I will render unto Babylon and to all the inhabitants of Chaldea all their evil that they have done in Zion in your sight, saith Jehovah. Behold, I am against thee, O destroying mountain, saith Jehovah, which destroyest all the earth; and I will stretch out my hand upon thee, and roll thee down from the rocks and will make thee a <u>burnt mountain</u>. And they shall not take of thee a stone for a corner, nor a stone for foundations; but thou shalt be desolate for ever, saith Jehovah."

Comment: God will bring about something that destroys all humans and animals. The burnt mountain could be a description of a mushroom cloud. The stones will be so contaminated that they will never be used again.

> *Revelation 18:9-10 "And the kings of the earth, who committed fornication and lived wantonly with her, shall weep and wail over her, when they look upon the smoke of her burning, <u>standing afar off for the fear</u> of her torment, saying, Woe, woe, the great city, Babylon, the strong city! for in <u>one hour</u> is thy judgment come."*

Comment: In today's world, people tend to rush in to help others who are facing a crisis or disaster. The news reporters normally rush in so they can film the disaster. In this case, the area could be radioactive, so that the world will be forced to stay away.

> *Revelation 18:14-19 "And the fruits which thy soul lusted after are gone from thee, and all things that were dainty and sumptuous are perished from thee, and men shall find them no more at all. The merchants of these things, who were made rich by her, shall stand afar off for the fear of her torment, weeping and mourning; saying, Woe, woe, the great city, she that was arrayed in fine linen and purple and scarlet, and decked with gold and precious stone and pearl! For in an hour so great riches is made desolate. And every shipmaster, and every one that saileth any wither, and mariners, and as many as gain*

their living by sea, <u>stood afar off</u>, and cried out as they looked upon the smoke of her burning, saying, What city is like the great city? And they cast dust on their heads, and cried, weeping and mourning, saying, Woe, woe, the great city, wherein all that had their ships in the sea were made rich by reason of her costliness! For in <u>one hour</u> is she made desolate."

Comment: People are unable to help her because her torment will affect them as well. A bomb is capable of causing total destruction in one hour. People will only see smoke coming out of what used to be a great city. The picture described here is of an actual physical place, not some economic or religious system.

Summary: Possibility of nuclear bomb

The destruction of Babylon does not keep strange wildlife from living there. The people see each others' faces go up in flames. This fire appears as a burnt mountain. It is a singular fire that consumes cities or a large area. People or news reporters are unable to go there because they are afraid of the area. They see the results from a distance. The merchants realize that they will no longer be selling their goods there. Everything is destroyed.

****

Fall of Babylon - Daniel 11:36-45

Many people believe this text refers to the antichrist. However, the problem with this is that the "time of trouble" described in Daniel 12:1 does not come until after the king comes to his end and no one helps him. This is unlike the antichrist ruler who has help from all over the world in going against Israel, and is then cast alive into the lake of fire.

Daniel 11:36-45 (1) And <u>the king shall do according to his will</u>; and he shall exalt himself, and magnify himself above every god, and shall speak marvelous things against the God of gods; and he shall prosper till the indignation be accomplished; for that which is determined shall be done. Neither shall he regard the gods of his fathers, nor the desire of women, nor regard any god, for he shall <u>magnify himself above all</u>. (2) But in his place shall he honor the <u>god of fortresses</u>; and a god whom his fathers knew not shall he honor with gold, and silver, and with precious stones, and pleasant things. And he shall deal with the strongest fortresses by the help of a foreign god: (3) <u>whosoever acknowledgeth him he will increase</u> with glory; and he shall cause them to rule over many, and shall divide the land for a price. (4) And at the time of the end shall the king of the south contend with him; and (5) the king of the north shall come against him like a whirlwind, with chariots, and with horsemen, and with many ships; (6) and he shall enter into the countries, and shall overflow and pass through. He shall enter also into the <u>glorious land</u>, and <u>many</u>

countries shall be <u>overthrown</u>; but these shall be delivered out of his hand: Edom, and Moab, and the chief of the children of Ammon. He shall stretch forth his hand also upon the countries, (7) and the land of <u>Egypt shall not escape.</u> But he shall have power over the treasures of gold and of silver, and over all the precious things of Egypt; (8) and the <u>Libyans and the Ethiopians</u> shall be at his steps. (9) But tidings out of the <u>east and out of the north shall trouble him</u>; and he shall go forth <u>with great fury</u> to destroy and <u>utterly to sweep away many.</u> (10) And he shall plant the tents of his palace between the <u>sea and the glorious holy mountain</u>; (11) yet he shall come to his end, and <u>none shall help him.</u>"

Comment by Numbers: (1) This king is accountable to no one. (2) His god is his military strength and he spends money on his military equipment so that he can stand against the strongest military. (3) Those who support him are given authority to help rule the land. (4) The "king of the south" could be from Saudi Arabia, and (5) the "king of the north" could be Kurdish. (6) He will go in and attack "the glorious nation," or Israel, and in his destruction he causes a "mortal wound" to the Arab world. In the process, Jordan will fall and is then controlled by Israel. (7) Egypt will not escape his control as can be seen during the Gulf War when most of the refugees fleeing Iraq were from Egypt and they had lost their jobs. Egypt also saw a loss of revenue then when the tourism busses were attacked. (8) Libya and Sudan verbally supported Iraq in the Gulf War. Following Iraq's example Libya was also making weapons of mass destruction. (9) Iran (to the east) and the Kurds (to the north) were gassed during his war with Iraq. (10) Saddam hid his military weapons in the desert between the Persian Gulf and Israel. (11) When has one king stood against the whole world alone? If this passage refers to Saddam Hussein he did come to his end with no help. This king is before the time of trouble that follows in Daniel, Chapter 12.

<u>Summary: Daniel 11:36-45</u>

During the end times, we know from the book of Revelation that there are three distinct identities in the final battle of Armageddon. We need to be careful not to tie all of Daniel's visions into one person (the antichrist). Daniel saw them separately and would have told us if they were the same. Daniel saw the last king of Daniel chapter 11 as coming to his end with no help given to him from other kings. After this king comes to an end, Daniel is told the worst time of trouble that will ever be is coming. It is possible this king was Saddam Hussein as he spent the wealth of his country on military equipment. As news came from the East (Iran) and also the north (Kurds), he did go forth with great fury using his weapons of mass destruction to kill those opposed to him. The only two countries that supported him verbally during the Gulf War were Libya and Sudan (Ethiopia). He also used attacks against Israel to try and bring the Arabs on his side. He received no help from any other nation.

****

The End Result of the Fall

Isaiah 14:7-9 "the whole <u>earth is at rest, and is</u>
<u>quiet: they break forth into singing</u>. Yea, the fir-
trees rejoice at thee, and the cedars of Lebanon,
saying, since thou art laid low, no hewer is come
up against us. <u>Sheol from beneath is moved</u> for
thee to meet thee at thy coming; it stirreth up the
dead for thee, even all the chief ones of the
earth; it hath raised up from their thrones all the
kings of the nations."

Comment: The whole earth is happy and quiet as evil is put in place and man sees the results of evil. People see how destructive the evil forces have been and how they have affected the whole world. Peace comes to the Middle East. The event is known in Sheol.

Revelation 18:20 "Rejoice over her, thou heaven,
and ye saints, and ye apostles, and ye prophets;
for <u>God hath judged your judgment on her</u>."

Comment: There is rejoicing in heaven and on earth among God's people. They rejoice because God has given Babylon what she deserved. They had experienced the wickedness of Babylon during their lives.

Revelation 19:1-5 "After these things I heard as
it were a great voice of a great multitude in
heaven, saying, Hallelujah; Salvation, and glory,
and power, belong to our God: for true and
righteous are his judgments; for he hath judged
the great harlot, her that corrupted the earth with
her fornication, and he hath avenged the blood

of his servants at her hand. And a second time they say, Hallelujah. And her smoke goeth up <u>forever and ever</u>. And the four and twenty elders and the four living creatures fell down and worshipped God that sitteth on the throne, saying, Amen; Hallelujah. And a voice came forth from the throne, saying, Give praise to our God, all ye his servants, ye that fear him, the small and the great."

Comment: Heaven and its hosts know of the destruction and that it is forever.

Isaiah 13:11-13 "And I will <u>punish the world</u> for their evil, and the wicked for their iniquity: and I will cause the arrogancy of the proud to cease, and will lay low the <u>haughtiness</u> of the terrible. I will make a man more rare than fine gold, even a man than the pure gold of Ophir. Therefore I will make the heavens to tremble, and the <u>earth shall be shaken out of its place</u>, in the wrath of Jehovah of hosts, and in the day of his fierce anger.

Comment: The fall of Babylon has a worldwide effect. Men will no longer boast in their own might. The earth will be shaken slightly out of its orbit, which will begin its wobbling described in **Isaiah, Chapter 24**. Also, the plagues of Revelation seem to be associated with the earth's orbit. This could to be the event that sets God's wrath in motion; an event that forever changes the earth's path, and it can never again be put back as it was.

> ***Jeremiah 50:46 "At the noise of the taking of Babylon the <u>earth trembleth</u>, and the <u>cry is heard among the nations.</u>"***

Comment: When the earth trembles, it affects the whole world. This can cause earthquakes, tidal waves, and many other natural disasters. The nations cry out as they experience the results of the earth trembling.

> ***Daniel 12:1 "And at that time shall Michael stand up, the great prince who standeth for the children of thy people; and there shall be a <u>time of trouble</u>, such as never was since there was a nation even to that same time: and at that time thy people shall be delivered, every one that shall be found written in the book."***

Comment: If Daniel, Chapter 11 refers to the king of Babylon, then after his end comes the beginning of the Tribulation. It is interesting to note in **Jeremiah 51:57** "And I will make drunk her princes and her wise men, her governors and her deputies, and her mighty men; and they shall sleep a perpetual sleep, and not wake, saith the King, whose name is Jehovah of hosts," there is no mention of the king of Babylon being present when the perpetual sleep begins for her rulers.

<u>Summary: The End Result of the Fall</u>

After the fall of Babylon is completed, the whole earth is at rest and happy as they can stop worrying about future wicked attacks. However, we also are told that with the fall of Babylon, the earth trembles and is shaken from its place. This would cause all kinds of natural disasters. I see this event as the key to changing the orbit of the earth. This path sets it on a new course, bringing on the plagues in the book of Revelation. Man will not be able to put earth back into its normal orbit. **Isaiah 24:5-6** and **Micah 7:13** tell us that the inhabitants of the earth have broken God's laws, bringing upon the earth its destruction.

We have no idea what could happen with a nuclear bomb exploding, with all the oil in that area. Also within the context of the fall of Babylon are the planets mentioned. **Isaiah 48:13** "Yea, my hand hath laid the foundation of the earth, and my right hand hath spread out the heavens: when I call unto them, they stand up together." The alignment of the planets affects the gravitational pull on earth. God laid out the foundation of the earth and when He calls them they stand up together. We also know those in Babylon include astrologers and stargazers. Could it be that Babylon's destruction comes at the exact moment when the planets are in alignment and the explosive forces pushing from the other side shift the earth slightly in its orbit?

****

The Fall of Babylon - The Announcing Angel

> *Revelation 14:8 "And another, <u>a second angel, followed</u>, saying, Fallen, fallen is Babylon the great, that hath made all the nations to drink of the wine of the wrath of her fornication."*

Comment: The angel announcing the fall of Babylon comes on the scene after completion of the first angel's message. When this future event happens, we will have a better understanding where to fit the fall into the sequence of end-time events. Mankind will also realize exactly how the first angel's was delivered to them.

Revelation 4:1 "After these things I saw, and behold, a door opened in heaven, and the first voice that I heard, a voice as of a trumpet speaking with me, one saying, Come up hither, and I will show thee the things which <u>must come to pass hereafter.</u>"

Comment: John is told at this point these will be future events. However, he is not told when they will begin.

Revelation 22:10 "And he saith unto me, Seal not up the words of the prophecy of this book; for the <u>time is at hand.</u>"

Comment: John is told at the end of the book of Revelation not to seal up the book. The reason given is that the time begins now. Therefore the fall of Babylon could happen anywhere in the book of Revelation before Christ's return.

Daniel 12:4 "But thou, O Daniel, shut up the words, and seal the book, even to the time of the end: <u>many shall run to and fro,</u> and <u>knowledge shall be increased.</u>"

Comment: Daniel is told to seal up the book until the time of the end. In other words, Daniel's message would not be understood until the end times. The sign that Daniel was given, of mankind running to and fro and knowledge being increased, is fitting for our time. The book of Daniel will be completely opened to our understanding soon.

> ***Revelation 18:1-3** "After these things I saw another angel coming down out of heaven, having <u>great authority</u>; and the earth was <u>lightened with his glory</u>. And he cried with a mighty voice, saying, Fallen, fallen is Babylon the great, and is become a habitation of demons, and a hold of every unclean spirit, and a hold of every unclean and hateful bird. For by the wine of the wrath of her fornication all the nations are fallen; and the kings of the earth committed fornication with her, and the merchants of the earthy waxed rich by the power of her wantonness."*

Comment: The two characteristics of the announcing angel are authority and enlightenment. Just as humans did not see the first angel, I doubt that we will see this announcing angel. However, we do know God's children will be involved in delivering the second angel's message. The Christians involved in this announcement will speak with the authority of fulfilled prophecies and also enlightenment about how the end times are being fulfilled. The fulfillment of the Old Testament prophecies of the fall of Babylon and those in the New Testament of Babylon will be the key that opens the eyes of the 144,000 Jews during the tribulation. They will realize that the prophecies of the Old Testament are the same as those in the New Testament; thus Jesus is the Messiah.

This angel's message causes us to reflect on the first angel's message.

Revelation 14:6-7 "And I saw another angel flying in mid heaven, having eternal good tidings to proclaim unto them that dwell on the earth, and unto every nation and tribe and tongue and people; and he saith with a great voice, Fear God, and give him glory; for the hour of his judgment is come: and worship him that made the heaven and the earth and sea and fountains of waters."

Comment: This angel's message began with Jesus, who began speaking it in **John 12:31** "Now is the judgment of this world: now shall the prince of this world be cast out." Jesus gave us the command to take the message into the entire world. As we look at history from the time of Christ, we realize God's message is going to every tribe, nation, and tongue. We physically have not seen an angel flying around delivering this message; Christ's followers are delivering the message today. With the fall of Babylon we will know exactly how this first message was delivered to mankind. As a child, God called me to serve Him full time in spreading His message. He used the story of the five missionaries killed by the Acura Indians in Ecuador to inspire me.

Revelation 14:1-5 "And I saw, and behold, the Lamb standing on the mount Zion, and with him a hundred and forty and four thousand, having his name, and the name of his Father, written on their foreheads. And I heard a voice from heaven, as the voice of many waters, and as the voice of a great thunder: and the voice which I *heard was as the voice of harpers harping with their harps: and they sing as it were a new song before the throne, and before the four living creatures and the elders: and no man could learn the song save the hundred and forty and four thousand, even they that had been purchased out of the earth. These are they that were not defiled with women; for they are virgins. These are they that follow the Lamb whithersoever he goeth. These <u>were purchased</u> from among men, to be the <u>first fruits unto God</u> and unto the Lamb. And in their mouth was found no lie: they are <u>without blemish.</u>*"

Comment: Involved in the first angel's message are the 144,000. This is a puzzling unit until you realize that they are standing with Jesus on Mount Zion and also that they were the first fruits among men purchased unto God. In the scriptures, the first fruits were sacrificed on the altar. I feel this is an announcement to us of those who are called to be martyrs for the cause of Christ during the Church Age. They are a unique group in that they share the experience of giving their lives rather then deny Christ. Also, I believe that these are the souls underneath the altar in **Revelation 6:9-11**. They are told to rest a little while until the next group like them should be killed. I feel the next group is the 144,000 Jews of **Revelation 7:4** who are chosen to give out the message of the third angel in **Revelation 14:9-11**.

<u>Summary: The Announcing Angel</u>

With the fall of Babylon, we will have a key piece of the prophetic puzzle in place. It will reveal how the first angel's message in Revelation, Chapter 14 was delivered to mankind. It will give great illumination to those seeking to understand God's message about Babylon. It will give them great authority when sharing the message with fellow humans. This piece of the puzzle will connect the many verses of Babylon's fall into the sequence of events revealed by the prophets about the end times.

****

The Rapture of the Church

> *Daniel 12:1-2 "And at that time shall Michael stand up, the great prince who standeth for the children of thy people; and there shall be a time of trouble, such as never was since there was a nation even to that same time: and at that time thy people shall be delivered, every one that shall be found written in the book. And many of them that sleep in the dust of the earth shall awake, some to everlasting life, and some to shame and everlasting contempt."*

Comment: There are two passages that relate to the rapture which also relate to the fall of Babylon. In **Daniel, Chapter 12** we are told that with the end of the last king in Chapter 11 (the king of Babylon), there comes a time of trouble such as never has been before in the history of this earth. Also, deliverance comes at that time to those whose names are found written in the book. Many, but not all, will rise from the dead. This is a description of the rapture. Some of those raised will go to everlasting life, but some will go to face punishment. This passage does not contradict **I Thessalonians 4:14-18**, because those verses emphasize that those who have fallen asleep having faith in Christ will be reunited with those going up in the rapture, thus realizing their hope of everlasting life with God and their loved ones. **Daniel 12:1-2** is unique, as it adds that the unsaved during the Church Age that will be raised at the same time, with no comfort given with their resurrection. Their resurrection would be to Hades, not the lake of fire, which will come at the end of the tribulation

> *Revelation 19:6-9 "And I heard as it were the voice of a great multitude, and as the voice of many waters, and as the voice of mighty thunders, saying, Hallelujah: for the Lord our God, the Almighty, reigneth. Let us rejoice and be exceeding glad, and let us give the glory unto him: for the <u>marriage of the Lamb is come</u>, and his wife hath made herself ready. And it was given unto her that she should array herself in fine linen, bright and pure: for the fine linen is the righteous acts of the saints. And he saith unto me, Write, <u>Blessed are they that are bidden to the marriage supper of the Lamb</u>. And he saith unto me, these are true words of God."*

Comment: After the rejoicing in heaven over the judgment of Babylon in **Revelation 19:1-5**, the next event John sees is the marriage supper of the Lamb. The bride is ready and clothed in the righteous acts of the saints. The

Christians are blessed to be welcomed to the marriage supper, instead of enduring the tribulation events transpiring on the earth.

Summary: The Rapture of the Church

The rapture is the subject Christians are expectantly waiting for; the fall of Babylon may be an unexpected surprise. Care should be taken to pay attention to the literal message God has given concerning the context to those receiving it. There does seem to be a connecting link between the fall of Babylon and the rapture. The Scriptures seem to place the rapture after the fall. The followers of Christ will be delivered from God's wrath; however, they will know the time of trouble is coming.

****

The Mortal Wound

Jeremiah 49:19-21 "Behold, he shall come up like a lion from the pride of the Jordan against the strong habitation: for I will suddenly make them run away from it; and whoso is chosen, him will I appoint over it: for who is like me?and who will appoint me a time? And who is the shepherd that will stand before me? Therefore hear ye the counsel of Jehovah, that he hath taken against ___Edom___*; and his purposes, that he hath purposed against the inhabitants of Teman: Surely they shall drag them away, even the little ones of the flock; surely he shall make their habitation* *desolate over them. The <u>earth trembleth at the noise of their fall</u>; <u>there is a cry, the noise whereof is heard in the Red Sea</u>.*"

Jeremiah 50:44-46 "Behold, the enemy shall come up like a lion from the pride of the Jordan against the strong habitation: for I will suddenly make them run away from it; and whoso is chosen, him will I appoint over it: for who is like me? and who will appoint me a time?: and who is the shepherd that can stand before me? Therefore hear ye the counsel of Jehovah, that he hath taken against <u>Babylon</u>; and his purposes, that he hath purposed against the land of the Chaldeans: Surely they shall drag them away, even the little ones of the flock; surely he shall make their habitation desolate over them. <u>At the noise of the taking of Babylon the earth trembleth, and the cry is heard among the nations</u>."

Comment: Note here that the verses pertaining to the fall of Babylon are identical to those of the prophecies against Edom. The only difference in the end result is the area that is affected. From **Jeremiah 49:18** we realize that the destruction of Edom, like that of Babylon, has not happened, because there are people still living there; Edom is not yet like the destruction of Sodom and Gomorrah. It is possible that the events of these two prophecies transpire at the same time, as the Scriptures seem to connect these two passages with their wording. Israel is promised areas of land after the fall of Babylon that they do not enjoy today. For this to become a reality, a restructuring of the Middle East must take place.

Revelation 13:1-3 "and he stood upon the sand of the sea. And I saw a beast coming up out of the sea, having ten horns, and seven heads, and on his horns ten diadems, and upon his heads names of blasphemy. And the beast which I saw was like unto a leopard, and his feet were as the feet of a bear, and his mouth as the mouth of a lion: and the dragon gave him his power, and his throne, and great authority. And I saw one of his heads as though it had been smitten unto death; and his death-stroke was healed: and the whole earth wondered after the beast."

Comment: The ten horns hate the whore, which is Babylon. They make her desolate and burn her with fire **(Revelation 17:16)**. The ten horns have not received their kingdoms yet **(Revelation 17:12)**. "And the ten horns that thou sawest are ten kings, who have received no kingdom as yet; but they receive authority as kings, with the beast, for one hour." This same beast receives a mortal wound to one of its seven heads. It should be noted that the beast is in its near completed form when this happens. The seven heads and ten horns are in place, thus it could be any one of the seven that receives the mortal wound. We also know this beast is Israel's number one enemy. It is only through God's protection that Israel is allowed to survive.

Isaiah 48:5-6 "therefore I have declared it to thee from of old; before it came to pass I showed it thee; lest thou shouldest say, Mine idol hath done them, and my graven image, and my molten image, hath commanded them. Thou hast heard it; behold all this; and ye, will ye not declare it? I have showed thee new things from this time, even hidden things, which thou has not known".

Comment: God's deliverance is prophesied to them, but they have not heard it. God's prophecies are given to Israel so that when they are fulfilled, Israel will not be able to claim victory though her own strength. Thus, it is possible that the mortal wound to the beast is mentioned in the prophecies, but we just haven't seen the connection yet. Israel is told of her deliverance in the context of the fall of Babylon.

Jeremiah 49:34-39 "The word of Jehovah that came to Jeremiah the prophet concerning Elam, in the beginning of the reign of Zedekiah king of Judah, saying, Thus saith Jehovah of hosts: Behold, I will break the bow of Elam, the chief of their might. And upon Elam will I bring the four winds from the four quarters of heaven, and will scatter them toward all those winds; and there shall be <u>no nation whither the outcasts of Elam shall not come</u>. And I will cause Elam to be dismayed before their enemies, and before them that seek their life; and I will bring evil upon them, even my fierce anger, saith Jehovah; and I will <u>send the sword after them</u>, till I have consumed them; and I will set my throne in Elam, and will destroy from thence king and princes, saith Jehovah. But it shall come to pass in the <u>latter days,</u> that I will bring back the captivity of Elam, saith Jehovah."

Comment: This is another one of the prophecies written in the same style as those about Babylon that has no clear fulfillment, yet Elam is there in the latter days. Could it be that these prophecies that are written with the same style as that of Babylon happen at the same time? A possible explanation of this prophecy could be as follows: Babylon is destroyed by a massive atomic bomb. The wind carries the radioactive debris eastward over Elam, which is current day Iran. The people living there are contaminated. To get the necessary medical attention they will be sent to every country of the world. They will continue to die because they were exposed to radiation. However, after time has passed people will be allowed to return to their homes when the radiation is no longer a threat. A king is raised up (the little horn), before which three other kings fall. This prophecy could be a description of the mortal wound to one of the heads of the end-time beast.

Summary: The Mortal Wound

The Scriptures are clear that certain events will happen. God does not give all the exact details, as mankind would, then seek to change them. The mortal wound to one of the heads of the beast will identify the end-time beast. God has given various prophecies concerning those countries that are clearly part of the Nebuchadnezzar image. Interestingly, some of these have no historical record of having been completed. This is especially true in the prophecy of Elam, yet, at the same time, Elam is there in the latter days.

God tells Israel, in the context of the fall of Babylon, of their deliverance ahead of time, so when it comes to pass they will not be able to say they were delivered by their own strength. In Revelation, Chapter 17 we are told Babylon rides on the end-time beast. However this beast is not in its final form. Its 10 horns have not yet received kingdoms, but receive authority as kings, nonetheless. Also, it does not yet have a mortal wound to one of the heads. The 10 horns hate Babylon and expose her and burn her with fire. My conclusion is that the fall of Babylon causes the mortal wound to the former kingdom of Persia (Iran). It will also remove the power against Israel from the surrounding countries

****

The Fall of Babylon in the Book of Revelation

> *Revelation 14:8-10 "And another, a <u>second angel</u>, followed, saying, Fallen, fallen is Babylon the great, that hath made all the nations to drink of the wine of the wrath of her fornication. And another <u>angel, a third</u>, followed them, saying with a great voice, If any man worshippeth the beast and his image, and receiveth a mark on his forehead, or upon his hand, he also shall drink of the wine of the wrath of God, which is prepared unmixed in the cup of his anger; and he shall be tormented with fire and brimstone in the presence of the holy angels, and in the presence of the Lamb."*

Comment: The fall of Babylon happens before the third angel's announcement to the world about the mark of the beast. Thus it happens before the last three-and-one- half years of the tribulation.

Revelation 17:12; 16 "And the ten horns that thou sawest are ten kings, who have received <u>no kingdom as yet</u>; but they receive authority as kings, with the beast, for one hour. And the ten horns which thou sawest, and the beast, these shall hate the harlot, and shall make her desolate and naked, and shall eat her flesh, and shall burn her utterly with fire."

Comment: When the ten horns are involved in the destruction of Babylon, they do not have their kingdoms yet. Also the beast Babylon rides on has not received the mortal wound to one of its heads yet.

Revelation 19:1-8 "After these things I heard as it were a great voice of a great multitude in heaven, saying, Hallelujah; Salvation, and glory, and power, belong to our God: for true and righteous are his judgments; for he hath judged the great harlot, her that corrupted the earth with her fornication, and he hath avenged the blood of his servants at her hand. And a second time they say, Hallelujah. And her smoke goeth up for ever and ever. And the four and twenty elders and the four living creatures fell down and worshipped God that sitteth on the throne, saying, Amen; Hallelujah. And a voice came forth from the throne, saying, Give praise to our God, all ye his servants, ye that fear him, the small and the great. And I heard as it were the voice of a great multitude, and as the voice of *many waters, and as the voice of mighty thunders, saying, Hallelujah: for the Lord our God, the Almighty, reigneth. Let us rejoice and be exceeding glad, and let us give the glory unto him: for the <u>marriage of the Lamb is come</u>, and his wife hath made herself ready. And it was given unto her that she should array herself in fine linen, bright and pure: for the fine linen is the righteous acts of the saints."*

Comment: The fall of Babylon happens before the marriage of the Lamb, or before the rapture.

Revelation 16:17-21 "And the seventh poured out his bowl upon the air; and there came forth a great voice out of the temple, from the throne, saying, It is done: and there were lightnings, and voices, and thunders; and there was a great earthquake, such as was not since there were men upon the earth, so great an earthquake, so mighty. And the great city was divided into three parts, and the cities of the nations fell: and <u>Babylon the great was remembered in the sight of God</u>, to give unto her the cup of the wine of the fierceness of his wrath. And every island fled away, and the mountains were not found. And great hail, every stone about the weight of a talent, cometh down out of heaven upon men: and men blasphemed God because of the plague of the hail; for the plague thereof is exceeding great."

Comment: In the last judgment of Revelation, the earth receives the final fierceness of God's wrath. The word "remembered" should be noted. Here God's judgment against Babylon is complete. The sin of Babylon polluted the earth. Since Babylon was destroyed earlier, here God is remembering to judge and remove completely Babylon's influence upon the earth. This is necessary before He can set up His kingdom.

Isaiah 48:5-6 "therefore I have <u>declared it to thee</u> from of old; before it came to pass I showed it thee; lest thou shouldest say, Mine idol hath done them, and my graven image, and my molten image, hath commanded them. Thou hast heard it; behold all this; and ye, will ye not declare it? I have showed thee new things from this time, even hidden things, which thou hast not known."

Comment: In the context of the fall of Babylon and Israel's deliverance, Israel is told that they were told about this before it came to pass. They will not be able to say that they accomplished this on their own. Thus the events are found in the Scriptures. We just aren't told exactly where and how it fits together.

Revelation 4:1 "After these things I saw, and behold, a door opened in heaven, and the first voice that I heard, a voice as of a trumpet speaking with me, one saying, Come up hither, and I will show thee the things which must come to <u>pass hereafter</u>."

Comment: The hereafter could begin anytime after the time of John's writings.

Revelation 22:10 "And he saith unto me, <u>Seal</u> <u>not</u> up the words of the prophecy of this book; for the <u>time is at hand</u>."

Comment: John is told not to seal up Revelation because the time is about to begin.

Revelation 6:7-11 "And when he opened the fourth seal, I heard the voice of the fourth living creature saying, Come. And I saw, and behold, a <u>pale horse</u>: and he that sat upon him, his name was <u>Death; and Hades</u> followed with him. And there was given unto them authority over the fourth part of the earth, to <u>kill with sword</u>, and with <u>famine</u>, and with <u>death</u>, and by the <u>wild beasts of the earth</u>. And when he opened the fifth seal, I saw <u>underneath the altar the souls of them that had been slain</u> for the word of God, and for the testimony which they held: and they <u>cried with a great voice</u>, saying, How long, O Master, the holy and true, dost thou not judge and avenge our blood on them that dwell on the earth? And there was given them to each one a white robe; and it was said unto them, that they should rest yet for a little time, until their fellow-servants also and their brethren, who should be killed even as they were, should have fulfilled their course."

Comment: The place I see where the fall of Babylon, a disastrous event, would fit in Revelation, is with the fourth seal. The event comes before the fifth seal, where the martyrs are allowed to talk to God (the rapture). The same sequence is found in Chapter 19. It is interesting to note in the fourth seal that death and Hades followed the pale horse, signifying that seal affects mainly the unsaved world. I believe the pale horse is of a greenish color. It is interesting to note the flag of Palestine is green. I believe we are about to enter this fourth seal where we will see one-fourth of the world's population die. Remember the fall of Babylon affects the whole world. This raises the question that if this is true, what were the first three seals?

Revelation 6:1-6 "And I saw when the Lamb opened one of the seven seals, and I heard one of the four living creatures saying as with a voice of thunder, Come. And I saw, and behold, a white horse, and he that sat thereon had a bow; and there was given unto him a crown: and he came forth <u>conquering, and to conquer</u>. And when he opened the second seal, I heard the second living creature saying, Come. And another horse came forth, a red horse: and to him that sat thereon it was given to <u>take peace from the earth</u>, and that they should <u>slay one another</u>: and there was given unto him a great sword. And when he opened the third seal, I heard the third living creature saying, Come. And I saw, and behold, a black horse; and he that sat thereon had a balance in his hand. And I heard as it were a voice in the midst of the four living creatures *saying, A measure of <u>wheat</u> for a <u>shilling,</u> and three measures of <u>barley for a shilling;</u> and the oil and the wine hurt thou not.*"

Comment: I have come to the conclusion that the seals are historical periods or events that affect the earth before God's wrath is poured out. Seal one is the conquering of the New World (the conquistadors). Seal two is the World Wars, or the killing of one another. In the third seal, the emphasis is on the price of things. Everything is more expensive. "Not hurting of the oil and wine" shows that life is still good, but more expensive (difficult economic times).

Summary: The Fall of Babylon in The Book of Revelation

The Scriptures in the book of Revelation tell us of the fall of Babylon. They do not reveal exactly where it fits in the timeline of the overall events. We are told it happens before the warning announcement about the mark of the beast. We also are told she rides on the end-time beast before the 10 kingdoms are given to its heads, and before one of the heads receives a mortal wound. Her fall comes before the marriage of the Lamb in heaven.

The fall of Babylon affects the whole world with disastrous consequences. The place it seems to fit is in the fourth seal where a fourth part of the earth's population dies. This fits **Revelation 19:1-8** where the marriage of the Lamb comes after the fall of Babylon. The fifth seal states the martyrs are allowed to talk to God. The rapture brings them into His presence. Thus the fall of Babylon would have happened earlier. The end result of tribulation is that God remembers and removes all of Babylon's influence before He sets up His kingdom.

****

Conclusion Of The Fall Of Babylon

We find the beginning of the history of mankind in the country of Iraq. Located there was the Garden of Eden, the place where sin entered the world; the Tower of Babel, where false worship led God to confound man's one language into various languages; Nineveh, the place to which Jonah was sent to preach repentance from sin; and Noah's homeland, which was the target of God's punishment for sin when He sent the flood to wipe out all mankind except for Noah and his family.

The city of Babylon is mentioned almost as much as Jerusalem in the Bible. It is important for God to tell us about Babylon and how its influence has spread throughout the whole world.

Zechariah 5:8 "And he said, <u>This is Wickedness:</u> and he cast her down into the midst of the ephah; and he cast the weight of lead upon the mouth thereof." Zechariah 5:11 tells us that this woman, who is called Wickedness, is taken to Shinar, which is another name for Babylon. To understand Babylon, it is necessary to think in terms of wickedness. The Scriptures tell us that the love of money is the root of all evil. Through wickedness, Babylon obtains her desires and riches. We are told that Babylon is drunken with the blood of the saints and of the martyrs of

Jesus. They hate those that try to restrain evil. Follow the trail of those killed because of their loyalty to God and you will find the influence that Babylon has brought on the world.

This subject is one we need to study and watch as we see present day events unfold. Whether Babylon is represented by the country of Iraq or just the area around the town of Babylon, which still exists in Iraq today, is open to debate since God chose not to give us all the exact details. We know from the Scriptures that the fall of Babylon has not yet been completed. The events of our time more closely fit God's description of Babylon's fall than the historical events that have transpired in the past in that part of the world. Several years ago Saddam Hussein had a painting done showing himself and King Nebuchadnezzar as equals. This illustrates the direct connection of the old and new empires of Babylon.

The Scriptures about Israel that are found in the prophecies against Babylon are within the context of the fall of Babylon. God's descriptions of Israel and Babylon are not there just by accident, but are related to each other. God is using His chosen people of Israel to bring about the defeat of evil in this world. I believe the peace of Israel during the first three-and-a-half years of the tribulation will be made possible by defeat of Israel's enemies (the mortal wound to one of the heads of the beast). As Israel's enemies labor to destroy her off the face of the earth, their quest will ultimately lead to their downfall. Perhaps as they send off a nuclear bomb intended to wipe Israel off the face of the earth, it will explode on the launch pad.

In the fall of Babylon, Isaiah prophesied that the earth would be shaken from its place. Jeremiah prophesied that the earth will tremble and the cry will be heard among the nations. Trembling or shaking of the earth would cause major earthquake disasters worldwide and could even affect the earth's orbit. With all the oil under that area of the world we have no idea what a bomb would cause. **Isaiah 24:5** states that the earth is defiled by its inhabitants because they transgressed the laws, changed the ordinances, and broke the everlasting covenant. **Isaiah 24:6** states the curse devours the earth. **Micah 7:13** also states that the earth will become desolate because of what the inhabitants of earth do. As you look at Revelation, you realize that most of the plagues are directly related to the earth's orbit.

For Israel to enjoy the areas of land mentioned in the context of the fall of Babylon, Jordan, Syria, Palestine, and Lebanon would have to give up their control of those areas. Israel faces her hopeless situation and asks for God's help in **Jeremiah 50:4-5** "In those days, and in that time, saith Jehovah, the children of Israel shall come, they and the children of Judah together; they shall go on their way weeping, and shall seek Jehovah their God. They shall inquire concerning Zion with their faces thitherward, *saying*, Come ye, and join yourselves to Jehovah in an everlasting covenant that shall not be forgotten." Pay attention, because God enjoys showing His power in hopeless situations. The way I see it happening is that Israel will be attacked by the Arab Muslim world. Jordan, Syria, Palestine, and Lebanon will fall, allowing Israel to control the areas promised to them and also allowing them to rebuild their temple. In the process, Babylon, or the central part of Iraq, is destroyed and contaminated by a nuclear bomb and is never to be inhabited again. The radiation drifts over Iran, causing their people to be evacuated to all countries of the world in order to get the medical help they need. The result of this disaster shakes the earth out of its normal orbit, setting it on a new course. This disaster opens the fourth seal of **Revelation 6:7-8**, which results in one-fourth of the world's population dying. Israel has tried to make peace with its enemies, but they have refused and attempted to wipe Israel off the face of the earth. Israel will have a peace agreement with the world allowing them to keep the land they captured. The peace will only last three-and-a-half years, until Iran returns to its country and then begins the process of bringing the world to the Battle of Armageddon.

We are told in Revelation that the ten horns expose and burn with fire the harlot of Babylon. In the prophecies of the fall of Babylon, two of these horns are mentioned. They are Media (the Kurds) and Elam (Iran). The common factor in these areas is the Muslim religion. I believe the ten horns come out of the Muslim Arab world. They are the clay of the Nebuchadnezzar image. What came out of the Roman Empire (the iron) is Catholicism. I believe one of the popes will be the false prophet mentioned in Revelation, Chapter 13. When you put the Catholics (iron) and the Muslims (clay) together, you get the partly weak, partly strong feet of Nebuchadnezzar's image. If you put the Catholic and the Muslim religions together, you have over half the world's population. It is interesting to note the end times' power could come in the name of democracy. We know from the Scriptures that many more are on the road to destruction than the road to heaven. Thus we can be outvoted at any time.

I see Revelation as a survival guide for believers, keeping their faith strong. With the fall of Babylon, God's message to mankind changes to one of His coming wrath. The message of the fall of Babylon will divide those that believe in God from those who follow selfish desires and the devil. We certainly live in exciting times and we see God's Word, which was written several thousand years ago, describe the events of today. Daniel 12:10 states that the wicked will do wickedly and not understand, but the wise shall understand.

The Fall Of Babylon

Chapter Four

Finishing the Seals

The Fall of Babylon brings on the sixth and seventh seals. It also sets in motion the coming of the plagues found in the book of Revelation.

Sixth Seal

> *Revelation 6:12-17 "And I saw when he opened the sixth seal, and there was a great earthquake; and the sun became black as sackcloth of hair, and the whole moon became as blood; and the <u>stars of the heaven fell unto the earth</u>, as a fig tree casteth her unripe figs when she is shaken of a great wind. And the heaven was removed as a scroll when it is rolled up; and <u>out every mountain and island were moved of their places.</u> And the kings of the earth, and the princes, and the chief captains, and the rich, and the strong, and every bondman and freeman, <u>hid themselves</u> in the caves and in the rocks of the mountains; and they say to the mountains and to the rocks, Fall on us, and hide us from the face of him that*

sitteth on the throne, and from the wrath of the Lamb: for the great day of their wrath is come; and who is able to stand?"

Comment: The stars falling on the earth and causing a great earthquake mark this period of time. The dust darkens the sun and moon. The stars arrive in quantities. It is noted that every one is hiding in the caves and among the rocks. Thus, they knew ahead of time about the coming disaster. With the fall of Babylon, the earth is shaken out of its place and set on a new course leading to collisions with the stars. The people want death because they are unable to endure or change the situation. The world as we know it will be changed as every mountain and island is moved out of its place. At this point, people realize the day of God's wrath has come. This is perhaps the arrival of Satan and his angels. **Revelation 12:7-9** states that they are cast out of heaven to earth when they lose the battle with Michael and his angels. **Revelation 12:4** refers to Satan drawing one-third part of the stars and casting them to earth. Satan and his angels will have lost their glory; thus, they will arrive as dark stars.

Seventh Seal

Revelation 8:1-5 "And when he opened the seventh seal, there followed a silence in heaven about the space of half an hour. And I saw the seven angels that stand before God; and there were given unto them seven trumpets. And another angel came and stood over the altar, having a golden censer; and there was given unto him much incense, that he should add it *unto the <u>prayers of all the saints</u> upon the golden altar which was before the throne. And the smoke of the incense, with the prayers of the saints, went up before God out of the angel's hand. And the angel taketh the censer; and he filled it with the fire of the altar, and cast it upon the earth: and there followed thunders, and voices, and lightnings, and an earthquake."*

Comment: Even though there is silence, it still reveals God and what is happening. **Habakkuk 2:20** "But Jehovah is in his holy temple: let all the earth keep silence before him" illustrates this scene. The absence of noise reveals that Satan has already been cast out. He is no longer there accusing the brethren day and night as **Revelation 12:10** states he does. Also, with this silence we realize that the followers of Christ are silent. They are not complaining or asking God the why questions, or excusing their shortcomings. They see their past prayers (many of which were difficult) mixed with incense and offered on the altar before God. They will understand God's work and the part their prayers have played. The most significant aspect of this silence is that God is silent. He isn't preaching to the saints about what they should have done or how badly they have lived, thus illustrating **Romans 8:1**, which states that there is no condemnation to those who are in Christ Jesus. When the fire from the altar was cast upon the earth there followed thunders, voices, lightening, and earthquake. This represents God's direct presence as referenced in **Revelation 4:5, Revelation 11:19, Revelation 16:18, Exodus 19:16, Matthew 24:27,** and **Luke 17:24.**

Revelation 7:1-8 "After this I saw four angels standing at the four corners of the earth, holding the four winds of the earth, that <u>no wind should blow on the earth</u>, or on the sea, or upon any tree. And I saw another angel ascend from the sunrising, having the seal of the living God: and he cried with a great voice to the four angels to whom it was given to hurt the earth and the sea, saying, <u>Hurt not the earth</u>, neither the sea, nor the trees, <u>till we</u> shall <u>have sealed the servants</u> of our God on their foreheads. And I heard the number of them that were sealed, a hundred and forty and four thousand, sealed out of every tribe of the children of Israel: Of the tribe of Judah were sealed twelve thousand:
Of the tribe of Reuben twelve thousand;
Of the tribe of Gad twelve thousand;
Of the tribe of Asher twelve thousand;
Of the tribe of Naphtali twelve thousand;
Of the tribe of Manasseh twelve thousand;
Of the tribe of Simeon twelve thousand;
Of the tribe of Levi twelve thousand;
Of the tribe of Issachar twelve thousand;
Of the tribe of Zebulun twelve thousand;
Of the tribe of Joseph twelve thousand;
Of the tribe of Benjamin were sealed twelve thousand."

Comment: While the seventh seal brings silence in heaven, it is reflected on the earth as well. It is the calm after the storm of the stars falling on the earth. There is no wind as the earth once again begins its new rotation and directions.

Also, God's message on earth is silent until the one hundred forty four thousand Jews are chosen. These Jews will reflect on the prophecies of the Old Testament and also those of the New Testament plus the new world events. They will realize that the prophecies of the fall of Babylon found in the Old and New Testament are the same and that Jesus is the Messiah. They are sealed into God's family and will carry out God's message to the world. They will warn the world not to follow the devil by taking the mark of the beast, which will lead to their being cast into the lake of fire. The seal on their foreheads indicates the world identifies them as God's followers. Satanic forces will not be able to change their commitment to God. As a result of their witness, there will be a large group of believers that cannot be numbered. They will be from every nation and language. However, they must endure the evil forces of the tribulation to the point of laying down their lives. This is the second group of martyrs that the martyrs of the fifth seal are told to wait for. This group will also serve God in His temple and God will wipe away their tears, giving them eternal life.

Results of the One Hundred and Forty Four Thousand Jews' Message

> *Revelation 7:9-17 "After these things I saw, and behold, a great multitude, which no man could number, out of <u>every nation and of</u> all <u>tribes and peoples and tongues</u>, standing before the throne and before the Lamb, arrayed in <u>white robes</u>, and palms in their hands; and they cry with a great voice, saying, Salvation unto our God who sitteth on the throne, and unto the Lamb. And all the*

angels were standing round about the throne, and about the elders and the four living creatures; and they fell before the throne on their faces, and worshipped God, saying, Amen: Blessing, and glory, and wisdom, and thanksgiving, and honor, and power, and might, be unto our God for ever and ever. Amen. And one of the elders answered, saying unto me, These that are arrayed in white robes, who are they, and whence came they? And I say unto him, My lord, thou knowest. And he said to me, These are they that come of the great tribulation, and they washed their robes, and made them white in the <u>blood of the Lamb</u>. Therefore are they before the throne of God; and they serve him day and night in his temple: and he that sitteth on the throne shall spread his tabernacle over them. They shall <u>hunger no more, neither thirst any more; neither shall the sun strike upon them, nor any heat</u>: for the Lamb that is in the midst of the throne shall be their shepherd, and shall guide them unto fountains of waters of life: and <u>God shall wipe away every tear</u> from their eyes. "

Comment: They deliver God's message to every nation, tongue, and people group. These accept the blood of the Lamb as God's sacrifice for their sins. They have white robes indicating they are killed during the tribulation. In heaven they will no longer experience hunger from not being able to buy food because they refused to receive the mark of the beast, and will no longer be thirsting because of the polluted water. They also experienced the sun scorching them during the great tribulation. The misery of the great tribulation is gone as they enjoy worshiping God. They serve God continually in his temple.

Summary: The Seals

These events were still future when John wrote the book of Revelation.

Revelation 5:4-9 "And I wept much, because no one was found worthy to open the book, or to look thereon: and one of the elders saith unto me, Weep not; behold, the Lion that is of the tribe of Judah, the Root of David, hath overcome to open the book and the seven seals thereof. And I saw in the midst of the throne and of the four living creatures, and in the midst of the elders, a Lamb standing, as though it had been slain, having seven horns, and seven eyes, which are the seven Spirits of God, sent forth into all the earth. And he came, and he taketh it out of the right hand of him that sat on the throne. And when he had taken the book, the four living creatures and the four and twenty elders fell down before the Lamb, having each one a harp, and golden bowls full of incense, which are the prayers of the saints. And they sing a new song, saying, Worthy art thou to take the book, and to open the seals thereof: for thou was slain, and didst purchase unto God with thy blood men of every tribe, and tongue, and people, and nation."

Only Jesus is worthy to open the seals. He is the Creator and Sustainer of this earth. The Scriptures tell us God controls the rulers of this world. The seals are events Jesus has planned. My conclusion is that these are historical periods that come upon this earth. These events bring us humans to recognize His dominion and that He is worthy of our praise. He is preparing us for His kingdom. However, Satan continues his battle, blinding the eyes of the unsaved, so that they will not believe.

****

The Timeline of Revelation

The timeline of future events in the book of Revelation seems to chronologically be in order through Chapter 11. At this point, the kingdoms of this world become God's Kingdom. After Chapter 11, time is spent identifying the major players in the events and filling in the details. The warfare in Revelation has its roots all the way back to the Garden of Eden, when man chose to eat of the tree of knowledge of good and evil. God's love for His creation caused Him to provide a way of deliverance. This did not end the struggle mankind experiences between good and evil. Mankind today continues to pay the consequences of his deeds. The battle continues between God and Satan and their followers. On this earth, the souls of men are the centerpiece of this battle. God desires to lead mankind to truth and enjoyment of His Kingdom. Satan seeks to destroy God's creation. This battle continues until the very end of this present earth. On Satan's side during the tribulation, his unholy trinity will be manifested through Satan himself, the ten-horned beast, and the false prophet. We know this because the sixth bowl states these three distinct identities sent out representatives to bring the world against Israel, God's chosen people.

The Fall Of Babylon

Chapter Five

The Trumpets and the Bowls

There seems to be a relationship between these two series of separate events. In some ways they are similar in nature. It appears to me they are cause and effect events. The trumpets are more announcements, followed by the events. The bowls are more of a pouring out event, causing the disasters of the trumpets to spread. We know that they happen during the same time period because they both end with Christ defeating his enemies and His Kingdom coming to this world. The seven wraths of God seem to be announced and delivered to the inhabitants of this world by the two witnesses in **Revelation 11:3-6.**

Number One Trumpet and Bowl

   Trumpet One

> *Revelation 8:6-7 "And the seven angels that had the seven trumpets prepared themselves to sound. And the first sounded, and there followed <u>hail and fire</u>, <u>mingled with blood</u>, and they were cast*

upon the earth: and the third part of the earth was burnt up, and the third part of the trees was burnt up, and all green grass was <u>burnt up</u>."

Comment: After the stars fall on the earth there is the calm of the Seventh Seal, with no wind blowing. However, the falling stars striking the earth will affect the earth's rotation and the weather patterns. Plus, the pollution in the air, caused by the stars falling, falls back to earth. This causes severe weather storms and pollution like acid rain that kills plant life.

Bowl One

Revelation 16:1-2 "And I heard a great voice out of the temple, saying to the seven angels, Go ye, and pour out the seven bowls of the wrath of God into the earth. And the first went, and poured out his bowl into the earth; and it became a noisome and <u>grievous sore</u> upon <u>the men that had the mark of the beast</u>, and that worshipped his image."

Comment: The air pollution causes reactions in humans. As they endure the first trumpet experience those who have the mark of the beast will be affected. The mark of the beast (number of man **Revelation 13:18**) will probably be an implanted chip. Perhaps the pollution causes a chemical reaction with the chip making a sore that will not heal.

Number Two Trumpet and Bowl
Trumpet Two

Revelation 8:8 "And the second angel sounded, and as it were a great mountain burning with fire was cast into the sea: and the third part of the sea became blood;"

<u>Comment:</u> The burning mountain sounds like a meteorite coming through the earth's atmosphere. It strikes the ocean, destroying one-third of the sea life and one-third of the ships - a direct hit that affects one-third of the ocean immediately.

Bowl Two

Revelation 16:3 "And the second poured out his bowl into the sea; and it became blood as of a dead man; and every living soul died, even the things that were in the sea."

<u>Comment:</u> The ocean spreads, contaminated from the burning mountain striking it. This causes all life in the sea to die. The dead bodies end up affecting all of the ocean waters.

Number Three Trumpet and Bowl
Trumpet Three

Revelation 8:10-11 "And the third angel sounded, and there fell from heaven a great star, <u>burning as a torch</u>, and it fell upon the third part of the rivers, and upon the fountains of the waters; and the name of the star is called Wormwood: and the third part of the <u>waters became wormwood</u>; and many men died of the waters, because they were <u>made bitter.</u>"

Comment: The star described as a torch reminds us of a comet. Because the earth's orbit will have been changed, we today have no idea which comet that might be. As the earth passes through the comet's tail the fresh water is polluted. The fact that it affects one-third of the fresh water shows that it puts a direct pollution into a third part of the fresh water, causing many to die from the water they drink.

Bowl Three

> *Revelation 16:4-7 "And the third poured out his bowl into the <u>rivers and the fountains of the waters;</u> and it became blood. And I heard the angel of the waters saying, Righteous art thou, who art and who wast, thou Holy One, because thou didst thus judge: for <u>they poured out the blood of the saints and the prophets,</u> and blood hast thou given them to drink: they are worthy. And I heard the altar saying, Yea, O Lord God, the Almighty, true and righteous are thy judgments."*

Comment: As the polluted, formerly fresh water flows and mixes with the rest of the fresh water, it causes it to become contaminated, turning red like blood. Those forced to drink this water are those who have killed God's people. By this time, mankind has learned how to treat the polluted water, so it does not kill men as with the third trumpet.

Number Four Trumpet and Bowl
Trumpet Four

Revelation 8:12-13 "And the fourth angel sounded, and the <u>third part</u> of the <u>sun was smitten</u>, and the third part of <u>the moon</u>, and the third part of <u>the stars</u>; that the third part of them should be darkened, and the <u>day should not shine for the third part</u> of it, and the <u>night in like manner</u>. And I saw, and I heard an eagle, flying in mid heaven, saying with a great voice, Woe, woe, woe, for them that dwell on the earth, by reason of the other voices of the trumpet of the three angels, who are yet to sound."

Comment: A third part of the sun, moon, stars, day and night are smitten, meaning they no longer exist. The cause for all these things being shortened can be explained if the rotation of the earth is speeded up, causing them to happen more frequently with shorter duration.

Bowl Four

Revelation 16:8-9 "And the fourth poured out his bowl upon <u>the sun</u>; and it was given unto it <u>to scorch men with fire</u>. And men were scorched with great heat: and they blasphemed the name of God who hath the power over these plagues; and they repented not to give him glory."

Comment: The earth speeds up its rotation because its path takes it closer to the sun. The people are scorched with great heat. The orbit around the sun during the tribulation will be changed due to the fact that the sun is darkened at the end of the tribulation. It is possible that before the earth leaves the sun's orbit it speeds up and makes a closer pass to the sun.

Number Five Trumpet and Bowl
Trumpet Five

Revelation 9:1-12 "And the fifth angel sounded, and I saw a star from heaven fallen unto the earth: and there was given to him the key of the pit of the abyss. And he opened the pit of the abyss; and there went up a smoke out of the pit, as the smoke of a great furnace; and <u>the sun and the air were darkened by reason of the smoke</u> of the pit. And out of the smoke came forth <u>locusts</u> upon the earth; and power was given them, as the scorpions of the earth have power. And it was said unto them that they should not hurt the grass of the earth, neither any green thing, neither any tree, but only such men as have not the seal of God on their foreheads. And it was given them that they should not kill them, but that they should be tormented five months: and their torment was as the torment of a scorpion, when it striketh a man. And in those days men shall seek death, and shall in no wise find it; and they shall desire to die, and death fleeth from them. And the shapes of the locusts were like unto horses prepared for war; and upon their heads as it were crowns like unto gold, and their faces were as men's faces. And they had hair as the hair of women, and their teeth were as teeth of lions. And they had breastplates, as it were

**breastplates of iron; and the sound of their wings
was as the sound of chariots, of many horses
rushing to war. And they have tails like unto
scorpions, and stings; and in their tails is their
power to hurt men five months. They have over
them as king the <u>angel of the abyss</u>: his name in
Hebrew is Abaddon, and in the Greek tongue he
hath the name <u>Apollyon</u>. The first Woe is past:
behold, there come yet two Woes hereafter."**

Comment: This star striking the earth opens the pit to the
abyss. The locusts go after people who are not God's
followers. The word abyss is the same as the one used in the
Gospel of Mark where the demons begged Jesus not to send
them there. In that story we know the demons possessed the
pigs and caused them to run into the sea. The locusts in
Revelation are demons controlled by their king, Satan, who
possesses them. Coming from the abyss they are used to living
in darkness. The men are living in darkness from the smoke
and the locusts are attacking them, causing intense pain. They
will wish they were dead, but will be unable to find death.
Demon-possessed people in the Bible did not kill themselves,
even though they harmed their bodies.

Bowl Five

**Revelation 16:10-11 "And the fifth poured out
his bowl upon the throne of the beast; and his
kingdom was darkened; and they gnawed their
tongues for pain, and they blasphemed the God
of heaven because of their <u>pains</u> and their <u>sores;</u>
and they <u>repented not</u> of their works. "**

Comment: The smoke from the pit of the abyss (with the fifth trumpet) darkens the kingdom of the beast. Men gnaw their tongues because of the pain from the locusts. They curse God because they are unable to stop the pain that they realize is from God. It should be remembered they still have sores from the first bowl. Still, they refuse to change and serve God.

Number Six Trumpet and Bowl

Trumpet Six

> *Revelation 9:13-21 "And the sixth angel sounded, and I heard a voice from the horns of the golden altar which is before God, one saying to the sixth angel that had one trumpet, Loose the four angels that are bound at the great <u>river Euphrates</u>. And the four angels were loosed, that had been prepared for the hour and day and month and year, that they should kill the <u>third part of men</u>. And the number of the armies of the horsemen was twice ten thousand times ten thousand: I heard the number of them. And thus I saw the horses in the vision, and them that sat on them, having breastplates as of fire and of hyacinth and of brimstone: and the heads of lions; and out of their mouths proceedeth fire and smoke and brimstone. By these three plagues was the third part of men killed, by the fire and the smoke and the brimstone, which proceeded out of their mouths. For the power of the horses is in their mouth, and in their tails: for their tails are like unto serpents, and have heads; and with them*

they hurt. And the rest of mankind, who were not killed with these plagues, repented not of the works of their hands, that they should not <u>worship demons, and the idols of gold, and of silver, and of brass, and of</u> <u>stone, and of wood</u>; which can neither see, nor hear, nor walk: and they repented not of their murders, nor of their sorceries, nor of their fornication, nor of their thefts."

Comment: This great army comes from the area around the River Euphrates. This is an indication of the area where the beast's powers are centered. One-third of men will be killed. This will be survival of the most wicked. Their lifestyle is one of worshipping demons. Their idols are of gold, silver, brass, stone and wood. The riches of this world drive them. They take their riches by murdering, stealing, trickery and committing fornication with wickedness.

Bowl Six

Revelation 16:12-16 "And the sixth poured out his bowl upon the great river, the river Euphrates; and the water thereof was dried up, that the <u>way</u> might be <u>made ready</u> for the kings that come <u>from the sunrising</u>. And I saw coming out of the mouth of the dragon, and out of the mouth of the beast, and out of the mouth of the false prophet, three unclean spirits, <u>as it were</u> <u>frogs</u>: for they are <u>spirits of demons</u>, working signs; which go forth unto the kings of the whole world, to gather them together unto the war of the great day of God, the Almighty. (Behold, I *come as a thief. Blessed is he that watcheth, and keepeth his garments, lest he walked naked, and they see his shame.) And they gathered them together into the place which is called in Hebrew Har-magedon."*

Comment: The drying up of the Euphrates River reveals where the main forces of the kings and armies are coming from against Israel. They are from east of the Euphrates River. This bowl reveals the three main adversaries against God and Israel. They are Satan, the beast and the false prophet. The representatives from these three are demon-possessed and go to the other countries of the world to bring them against the remaining Israelites in the battle of Armageddon. John describes them as frogs, no doubt because he saw them hopping by airplane from country to country. The closest comparison that he could come up with in his day was to describe them as frogs hopping all around.

Number Seven Trumpet and Bowl

Trumpet Seven

Revelation 11:14-19 "The second Woe is past: behold, the third Woe cometh quickly. And the seventh angel sounded; and there followed great voices in heaven, and they said, <u>The kingdom of the world is become the kingdom of our Lord, and of his Christ: and he shall reign forever and ever.</u> And the four and twenty elders, who sit before God on their thrones, fell upon their faces and worshipped God, saying, We give thee thanks, O Lord God, the Almighty, who art and *who wast; because thou hast taken thy great power, and didst reign. And the nations were wroth, and thy wrath came, and the time of the dead to be judged, and* **the time** *to give their* <u>reward to thy servants the prophets, and to the saints, and to them that fear thy name</u>, *the small and the great; and to destroy them that destroy the earth. And there was opened the temple of God that is in heaven; and there was seen in his temple the <u>ark of his covenant</u>; and there <u>followed lightnings, and voices, and thunders, and an earthquake, and great hail.</u>"*

Comment: With the sounding of the seventh trumpet, Christ receives His Kingdom. He destroys those who destroy His creation, the earth. God's people are resurrected to take their place in His Kingdom. The Ark of the Covenant is revealed in God's temple. God is with mankind. In the Scriptures when God is present, lightning, voices, and thunders evidence it. The earthquake and great hail indicate the trumpet's relationship with the seventh bowl and the battle of Armageddon.

Bowl Seven

Revelation 16:17-21 "And the seventh poured out his bowl upon the air; and there came forth a great voice out of the temple, from the throne, saying, It is done: and there were <u>lightnings, and voices, and thunders</u>; and there was a great earthquake, such as was not since there were men *upon the earth, so great an earthquake, so mighty. And the great city was divided into three parts, and the cities of the nations fell: and <u>Babylon the great was remembered</u> in the sight of God, to give unto her the cup of the wine of the fierceness of his wrath. And <u>every island fled away,</u> and <u>the mountains were</u> <u>not found.</u> And <u>great hail,</u> every stone about the weight of a talent, cometh down out of heaven upon men: and men blasphemed God because of the plague of the hail; for the plague thereof is exceeding great."*

Comment: God remembers the evil of Babylon, which is wickedness. All who have committed fornication with her are punished. This brings the end of God's wrath. The islands flee away and the mountains are not found, indicating the earth is returned to its original state before the flood. The great hail of one hundred pounds brings on God's winepress of **Revelation 14:20**. The earthquake is described in **Zechariah 14:4-5** *"And his feet shall stand in that day upon the mount of Olives, which is before Jerusalem on the east; and the mount of Olives shall be cleft in the midst thereof toward the east and toward the west, and there shall be a very great valley; and half of the mountain shall remove toward the north, and half of it toward the south. And ye shall flee by the valley of my mountains; for the valley of the mountains shall reach unto Azel; yea, ye shall flee, like as ye fled from before the earthquake in the days of Uzziah king of Judah; and Jehovah my God shall come, and all the holy ones with thee."* God provides an escape route.

Summary: Trumpets and Bowls

These events bring God's wrath upon this earth. His wrath has a physical affect on the earth, which in turn becomes disastrous for all mankind. If God did not shorten His wrath, no man would be left to enter His Kingdom. The trumpets and bowls in one way or another are related to the earth's orbit. At the fall of Babylon, the earth is shaken from its place. When this happens, man will be unable to stop the coming of God's wrath. Satan and his followers are angry with God and determined to silence His message. Even though they have power over God's people, it does not prevent the coming of God's Kingdom and their complete destruction.

****

The Seven Thunders
Within the context of the seven angels delivering God's wrath, there are seven thunders, which announce coming events.

Revelation 10:1-11 "And I saw another strong angel coming down out of heaven, arrayed with a cloud; and the <u>rainbow</u> was upon his head, and his face was as the <u>sun</u>, and his feet as <u>pillars of fire</u>; and he had in his hand a little book <u>open</u>: and he set his right foot upon <u>the sea, and his left upon the earth</u>; and he cried with a great voice, as a lion roareth: and when he cried, the seven thunders uttered their voices. And when the seven thunders uttered their voices, I was about to write: and I heard a voice from heaven saying, <u>Seal up the things which the seven thunders</u>

__uttered, and write them not.__ And the angel that I saw standing upon the __sea__ and upon the __earth__ lifted up his right hand to heaven, and sware by him that liveth for ever and ever, who created the heaven and the things that are therein, and the earth and the things that are therein, and the sea and the things that are therein, that there shall be delay no longer: but in the days of the voice of the seventh angel, when he is about to sound, then is finished the mystery of God, according to the good tidings which he declared to his servants the prophets. And the voice which I heard from heaven, I heard it again speaking with me, and saying, Go, take the book which is open in the hand of the angel that standeth upon the sea and upon the earth. And I went unto the angel, saying unto him that he should give me the little book. And he saith unto me, Take it, and __eat it__ up; and it shall make thy __belly bitter,__ but in thy __mouth it shall be sweet as honey.__ And I took the little book out of the angel's hand, and ate it up; and it was in my mouth sweet as honey: and when I had eaten it, my belly was made bitter. And they say unto me, Thou must prophesy again over many peoples and nations and tongues and kings."

Comment: This chapter begins by picturing how God led the children of Israel: The rainbow was a sign given to Noah that there would be no more destruction by flood. Moses' face was as the sun after being with God. The children of Israel were led at night by a pillar of fire.

This angel has a little book, which contains seven thunders. After the seven thunders utter, the book is sealed. During the tribulation the little book is open. This angel has his right foot on the sea and his left foot is on the earth. We know that out of the sea comes the ten-horned beast and out of the earth comes the false prophet. They oppose God and His people. It could be that the seven thunders are seven things that God leads his chosen people through. The mystery of God will be finished or known with the voice of the seventh angel. The little book to John was sweet as honey but to the stomach bitter. To me it means the seven thunders are seven things God's followers will experience through the tribulation from the false prophet and the beast. They will seem wonderful in the beginning, but end in bitter experiences. If these events had been written down, the believers would know what was coming next and would try to change their outcome.

The Two Witnesses

Revelation 11:1-13 "And there was given me a reed like unto a rod: and one said, Rise, and measure the temple of God, and the altar, and them that worship therein. And the <u>court</u> which is without the temple leave without, and <u>measure it not</u>; for it hath been <u>given unto the nations</u>: and the holy city shall they tread under foot forty and two months. And I will give unto my two witnesses, and they shall prophesy a thousand two hundred and threescore days, clothed in sackcloth. These are the two olive trees and the two candlesticks, standing before the Lord of the earth. And if any man desireth to hurt them, fire *proceedeth out of their mouth and devoureth their enemies; and if any man shall desire to hurt them, in this manner must he be killed. These have the power to shut the heaven, that it rain not during the days of their prophecy: and they have power over the waters to turn them into blood, and to smite the earth with every plague, as often as they shall desire. And when they shall have finished their testimony, the beast that cometh up out of the abyss shall make war with them, and overcome them, and kill them. And their dead bodies lie in the street of the great city, which spiritually is called Sodom and Egypt, where also their Lord was crucified. And from among the peoples and tribes and tongues and nations do men look upon their dead bodies three days and a half, and suffer not their dead bodies to be laid in a tomb. And they that dwell on the earth rejoice over them, and make merry; and they shall send gifts one to another; because these two prophets tormented them that dwell on the earth. And after the three days and a half the breath of life from God entered into them, and they stood upon their feet; and great fear fell upon them that beheld them. And they heard a great voice from heaven saying unto them, Come up hither. And they went up into heaven in the cloud; and their enemies beheld them. And in that hour there was a great earthquake, and the tenth part of the city fell; and there were killed in the earthquake seven thousand persons: and the rest were affrighted, and gave glory to the God of heaven."*

Comment: The temple in Jerusalem will be rebuilt, but the court outside will remain under the control of the nations. It is interesting to note that one of the present day plans for rebuilding the temple shows the Dome of the Rock and the courtyard still remaining. I feel that the rebuilding of the temple will be possible when the mortal wound happens to the Islamic countries. Israel will be allowed once again to have their nation freely. During the last three-and-one-half years of tribulation, the two witnesses will be God's representatives on earth. They will defend the temple during the time the saints are being killed because of their faith. They also deliver God's plagues on the earth. This is the reason the world rejoices over their being killed at the end.

The Fall Of Babylon

Chapter Six

Understanding the Warring Forces During the Tribulation

Biblical prophecies are directed toward a final result. In this case, the fact is that God is the victor and His kingdom will be established on this earth. One approach to understanding end-time prophecies is to take the end event and then work backwards, placing the earlier events around it. The Scriptures tell us that there will be an end-time battle where the nations of the world will be summoned together against God's people, Israel. The opposing forces at the center of this battle are God and Satan.

> ***Revelation 19:11-16** "And I saw the heaven opened; and behold, a white horse, and he that sat thereon called Faithful and True; and in righteousness he doth judge and make war. And his eyes **are** a flame of fire, and upon his head **are** many diadems; and he hath a name written*

which no one knoweth but he himself. And he is arrayed in a garment sprinkled with blood: and his name is called The Word of God. And the armies which are in heaven followed him upon white horses, clothed in fine linen, white and pure. And out of his mouth proceedeth a sharp sword, that with it he should smite the nations: and he shall rule them with a rod of iron: and he treadeth the winepress of the fierceness of the wrath of God, the Almighty. And he hath on his garment and on his thigh a name written, KINGS OF KINGS, AND LORD OF LORDS."

Comment: Jesus comes from heaven, followed by the armies of heaven. He is the one that treadeth the winepress, which is the wrath of God. This winepress is mentioned in **Joel 3:11-15** "Haste ye, and come, all ye nations round about, and gather yourselves together: thither cause thy mighty ones to come down, O Jehovah. Let the nations bestir themselves, and come up to the valley of Jehoshaphat; for there will I sit to judge all the nations round about. Put ye in the sickle; for the harvest is ripe: come, tread ye; for the winepress is full, the vats overflow; for their wickedness is great. Multitudes, multitudes in the valley of decision! for the day of Jehovah is near in the valley of decision. The sun and the moon are darkened, and the stars withdraw their shining".

Revelation 14:19-20. "And the angel cast his sickle into the earth, and gathered the vintage of the earth, and cast it into the winepress, the great **winepress,** *of the wrath of God. And the winepress are trodden without the city, and there* *came out blood from the winepress, even unto the bridles of the horses, as far as a thousand and six hundred furlongs".*

This passage reveals the blood will flow out of the winepress to the horse's bridles. The question is, how could this physically happen? The seventh trumpet and the seventh bowl tell us there will be great hail, as the kingdoms of this world will become Christ's Kingdom. These hailstones, weighing around one hundred pounds each, falling from the sky certainly will beat the armies gathered against God's people to a pulp. As the ice mixed with the blood melts it will flow out of the winepress just as the Bible states. It is very possible that horses will be present because the world as we know it will have changed. The supply of petroleum will be drastically affected by the plagues during the previous seven years. God wins this battle Himself - not Israel's armies. **Zechariah 14:4-5** tells us God provides a valley for them to flee to and escape.

Also, with this battle the Scriptures reveal details about Satan and his earthly forces. They are gathered together in a place called Armageddon, to bring the world armies together. **Revelation 16:13-14** reveals there are three identities that are the major controlling forces on the earth. They are the dragon, the beast and the false prophet. They send out their representatives to bring the world against Israel. We are told the representatives are really spirits of demons using signs to convince the world to eliminate Israel. Why is their going out referred to like frogs? It is possible that John saw them hopping around the world in airplanes. To him seeing a plane take off and land reminded him of frogs hopping from one place to another. We today use the term hopping from one country to another for representatives trying to form a peace agreement. It should be noted that the river Euphrates is dried up to make way for the kings of the east. Thus, the main army forces coming against Israel are from countries east of the Euphrates River. The country nearest is Iran. Presently they are Israel's number one enemy. No doubt they are part of the ten horns of the end-time beast. Next, we need to examine the three identities and their part in the war against God and His followers. These three identities are dealt with when Christ returns. The dragon (Satan) is chained for one thousand years. The beast and the false prophet are cast alive into the lake of fire. As we look backwards on the prophecies, we realize they are all leading up to this conclusion. Looking at how each ends up helps us understand the other visions that describe them. Thus we need to look at each identity to understand the part he plays in the end time.

End-Time Forces in the Book of Daniel

Prophecies found in the book of Daniel also reveal details of the end-time players. Daniel had a number of visions from God. His prophecies cover historical events all the way through to the end. His interpretation of Nebuchadnezzar's dream revealed the succession of kingdoms that God destroys to set up His Kingdom. It should be noted that Daniel remembers each of these visions and the angel who helped him understand it. We need to be careful not to lump all of these events into the same person (the antichrist) when Daniel sees them as separate visions. We should follow the clues and connect each vision with the identity revealed in Revelation. **Daniel, Chapter 7** reveals the four end time kingdoms in place when Christ returns. One of them is destroyed and burned with fire **(Daniel 7:11)**. **Daniel 7:12** reveals that the other three lose their dominion to Christ, but still continue for a season and a time. Thus these three are not part of the beast or the false prophet who are cast alive into the lake of fire. Since the first three beasts pass through the tribulation and we are fast approaching the end times, these beasts are probably present today.

Daniel 7:4 "The first was like a lion, and had <u>eagle's wings</u>: I beheld till the <u>wings thereof were plucked</u>, and it was lifted up from the earth, and made to <u>stand upon two feet as a man; and a man's heart was given to it.</u>"

Comment: The country which today is recognized by eagle's wings, is the United States. **Exodus 19:4** "Ye have seen what I did unto the Egyptians, and how I bare you on eagles' wings, and brought you unto myself," tells us God carried the children of Israel on eagle's wings from Egypt to the Promised Land. **Isaiah 40:31** "but they that wait for Jehovah shall renew their strength; they shall mount up with wings as eagles; they shall run, and not be weary; they shall walk, and not faint." We are told that when we wait for God, He will renew our strength and we will be carried along with wings of eagles. To me, Daniel is telling us that the eagle wings will be removed from the United States and will be made to stand up like a man with man's wisdom to guide it. Thus, this is the removal of God's blessing, which has carried the United States along, making it a great nation.

Daniel 7:5 "And, behold, another beast, a second, like to a <u>bear</u>; and it was raised up on *one side, and <u>three ribs</u> were in its mouth between its teeth: and they said thus unto it, Arise, <u>devour much flesh</u>."*

Comment: Today we recognize Russia as the bear. It would seem that only one side comes to power with three dominant parts, which causes the death of many people.

Daniel 7:6 "After this I beheld, and, lo, another, like a leopard, which had upon its back four wings of a bird; the <u>beast had also four heads</u>; and dominion was given to it."

Comment: This power has four dominant powers, which carry it along and give it dominion. To me, this seems to represent the European Common Market.

Daniel 7: 7-8 "After this I saw in the night-visions, and, behold, a fourth beast, terrible and powerful, and strong exceedingly; and it had great iron teeth; it devoured and brake in pieces, and stamped the residue with its feet: and it was diverse from all the beasts that were before it; and it <u>had ten horns</u>. I considered the horns, and, behold, there came up among them another horn, a little one, before which three of the first horns were plucked up by the roots: and, behold, in this horn were eyes like the eyes of a man, and <u>a mouth speaking great things</u>."

Comment: This beast with ten horns relates to the ten-horned beast in Revelation, Chapter 13. This ten-horned beast is the power that receives the mouth which blasphemies God. Daniel, Chapter 8 also refers to a little horn, which is present at the end-time events. However, Daniel does not connect this little horn to the little horn in Daniel, Chapter 7. The description in **Daniel 8:25** reveals this horn uses craft to destroy many and stands up against Christ, but is destroyed without human hand. This description connects it to the false prophet of Revelation, Chapter 13 who deceives mankind.

Daniel, Chapters 10 and 11 reveal another vision concerning future events. It should be noted this vision ends, and then in Daniel, Chapter 12 the beginning of a time of trouble which has never been experienced since the beginning of nations. Thus, this vision does not include the beast and the false prophet who are destroyed at Christ's return. I believe this vision ends with the fall of Babylon. It should be noted that Daniel is instructed to seal up these visions because they would not be known until the time of the end, when men will run to and fro and knowledge will be increased. Through Daniel's writings we know he desired to know the details of the end-time events. The events he saw caused him to be troubled and even become sick for several days. He is told to seal them up until the time of the end, when the wise would understand. The first identity we need to consider in the end time battle against Israel is the dragon. He is the one leading the rebellion, giving the beast and the false prophet the power to accomplish his work.

The Dragon

> *Revelation 12:9 "And the great dragon was cast down, the old serpent, he that is called the <u>Devil and Satan</u>, the deceiver of the whole world; he*

was cast down to the earth, and his angels were cast down with him."

Comment: We are told the dragon is the one we call Satan or the devil. The Bible also refers to him as the god of this world.

> *Revelation 12:3 "And there was seen another sign in heaven: and behold, a great red dragon, having <u>seven heads and ten horns</u>, and upon his heads <u>seven diadems.</u>"*

Comment: The devil is pictured as a dragon having seven heads with ten horns and seven crowns on these heads. From Daniel's prophecies we realize Satan will create this image of himself in the various kingdoms of this world down through history.

> *Revelation 12:4 "And his tail draweth the <u>third part of the stars of heaven</u>, and did cast them to the earth: and the dragon standeth before the woman that is about to be delivered, that when she is delivered he may devour her child."*

Comment: We are told he has control over a third part of the stars of heaven, and their allegiance to him causes them to be cast down to earth.

> *Revelation 12:7-9 "And there was <u>war in heaven:</u> Michael and his angels going forth to war with the dragon; and the dragon warred and his angels; And they prevailed not, neither was their*

place found any more in heaven. And the great dragon was cast down, the old serpent, he that is called the Devil and Satan, the deceiver of the whole world; he was cast down to the earth, and his angels were cast down with him."

Comment: The war Satan and his angels have with Michael and his angels results in Satan's defeat. Satan and his angels are cast down to earth. It is possible their arrival to this earth is found in **Revelation 6:13** "and the stars of the heaven fell unto the earth, as a fig tree casteth her unripe figs when she is shaken of a great wind."

Revelation 12:12-16 "Therefore rejoice, O heavens, and ye that dwell in them. Woe for the earth and for the sea: because the devil is gone down unto you, having great wrath, knowing that he hath but a short time. And when the dragon saw that he was cast down to the earth, he persecuted the woman that brought forth the man child. And there were given to the woman the two wings of the great eagle, that she might fly into the wilderness unto her place, where she is nourished for a time, and times, and half a time, from the face of the serpent. And the serpent cast out of his mouth after the woman water as a river, that he might cause her to be carried away by the stream. And the earth helped the woman, and the earth opened her mouth and swallowed up the river which the dragon cast out of his mouth."

Comment: Satan is angry upon his arrival and realizes he does not have much time left. Satan persecutes Israel and tries to destroy her with a flood of water but the earth opens up, allowing the water to go down. This flood is mentioned in **Daniel 9:26** "And after the threescore and two weeks shall the anointed one be cut off, and shall have nothing: and the people of the prince that shall come shall destroy the city and the sanctuary; and the end thereof shall be with a <u>flood,</u> and even unto the end shall be war; desolations are determined."

> *Revelation 12:17 "And the dragon waxed wroth with the woman, and went away to make war with the rest of her seed, that <u>keep the commandments of God</u>, and hold the testimony of Jesus."*

Comment: Satan seeks to destroy not only Israel, but also all those who keep God's commandments.

> *Revelation 13:2 "And the beast which I saw was like unto a leopard, and his feet were as the feet of a bear, and his mouth as the mouth of a lion: and the <u>dragon gave him his power, and his throne, and great authority.</u>"*

Comment: Satan gives the ten-horned beast its power and authority.

Summary: The Dragon

Even though humans will be unable to see the devil, we know he will have a human representative. We know this because **Revelation 16:13-14** states there are three representatives who go to the whole world to bring the countries to the final battle. My conviction is that Satan will be pictured to mankind in the form of the image of the beast that the false prophet causes to be made. The image is allowed to speak, causing the world to worship the image or be killed. **Revelation 13:14-15** "And he deceiveth them that dwell on the earth by reason of the signs which it was given him to do in the sight of the beast; saying to them that dwell on the earth, that they should make an image to the beast who hath the stroke of the sword and lived. And it was given *unto him* to give breath to it, *even* to the image to the breast, that the image of the beast should both speak, and cause that as many as should not worship the image of the beast should be killed." This image gives mankind a physical god to worship. The image also gives Satan the means to deliver his message to mankind. Satan, through the physical force from the ten-horned beast and the deception of the false prophet, will be able to communicate his message, allowing him control of the world as the god of it. I believe Satan's personal representative represents the image. This representative would be the little horn of Daniel, Chapter 7, which plucks up three of the ten horns. Thus, the ten-horned beast remains with only seven crowned horns and Satan's representative leads the other three horns as a separate unit, the core of Satan's force.

****

The Beast

Revelation 13:1 "and he stood upon the sand of the sea. And I saw a beast coming up out of the

***sea, having <u>ten horns</u>, and <u>seven heads</u>, and on
his <u>horns ten diadems</u>, and upon his <u>heads</u>
<u>names of blasphemy</u>.***"

<u>**Comment:**</u> The beast is identified by its seven heads with
ten horns and ten crowns. The beast comes out of the sea (sea
of mankind). In Daniel, Chapter 2 we are told of
Nebuchadnezzar's dream, which pictured the formation of an
image which is destroyed by Christ's return. We are told the
formation of the image describes kingdoms down through
history. **Revelation 13:1** also tells us the seven heads have
names of blasphemy. These heads are kingdoms, which did
not accept Israel as God's chosen people and placed their gods
over the Israelites instead of Jehovah. The Scriptures tell us of
the first two heads that blasphemed God in **Isaiah 52:4-5** "For
thus saith the Lord Jehovah, My people went down at the first
into <u>Egypt</u> to sojourn there: and the <u>Assyrian</u> hath oppressed
them without cause. Now therefore, what do I here, saith
Jehovah, seeing that my people is taken away for nought? they
that rule over them do howl, saith Jehovah, and my <u>name</u>
<u>continually all the day is blasphemed</u>."

Daniel has a vision, which he reveals in Daniel, Chapter
7, that includes four different beasts. The ten-horned beast is
number four, which God destroys with Christ's return. This
beast is cast alive into the lake of fire in **Revelation 19:20**
"And the beast was taken, and with him the false prophet that
wrought the signs in his sight, wherewith he deceived them
that had received the mark of the beast and them that
worshipped his image: they two were cast alive into the lake
of fire that burneth with brimstone." It should be noted the
other three beasts are allowed to live for a season and a time.
Daniel 7:12 "And as for the rest of the beasts, their dominion

was taken away: yet their <u>lives were prolonged</u> for a season and a time." Thus these three are not part of the Nebuchadnezzar image. **Revelation 13:2** "And the beast which I saw was like unto a <u>leopard</u>, and his feet were as *the feet* of a <u>bear</u>, and his mouth as the mouth of a <u>lion</u>: and the dragon gave him his power, and his throne, and great authority." This passage reveals certain ways that the ten-horned beast has characteristics similar to the other three beasts of Daniel, Chapter 7. Its body is patterned after the leopard, representing the third beast, possibly Europe. The feet are like those of the bear, representing the second beast, possibly Russia. These feet are used to destroy much flesh. The beast has a mouth like that of the lion, representing the first beast, possibly the United States. It tells the world of all its greatness. The ten-horned fourth beast is empowered by Satan and has great authority over the other three beasts.

Revelation 13:3 "And I saw <u>one of his heads</u> as though it had been <u>smitten unto death</u>; and <u>his death-stroke was healed</u>: and the whole earth wondered after the beast;"

Comment: One of the seven heads receives a mortal wound. It should be noted that at the time of the mortal wound, the beast is near its completed form. The seven heads, ten horns, and ten crowns are in place. The only thing lacking is the little horn before which three horns fall, leaving seven crowns. Thus the mortal wound could be to any one of the seven heads (empires which have ruled over Israel).

Revelation 13:4 "and they <u>worshipped the dragon</u>, because he gave his <u>authority unto the</u>

beast; and they worshipped the beast, saying, Who is like unto the beast? And who is able to war with him?"

Comment: The dragon gives power to the beast, which is the mouth of the image. This power causes the people to worship Satan. The world realizes this kingdom is not one that they can defeat.

Revelation 13:5-6 "and there was given to him a mouth speaking great things and blasphemies; and there was given to him authority to continue forty and two months. And he opened his mouth for blasphemies against God, to blaspheme his name, and his tabernacle, even them that dwell in the heaven."

Comment: The mouth given to the beast comes at the middle of the tribulation. It seems this is when the image is given breath to speak and is placed in the temple as god, thus blaspheming Jehovah and His rightful place of worship. Satan now has a mouth to deliver his message and a way for people to worship him. The beast places itself above and against God. The mouth reveals the message that those who do not worship the image of the beast should be killed. No one can buy or sell without receiving the mark. Also this mouth blasphemes those who dwell in the heaven. Satan is the one who knows about heaven.

Revelation 13:7 "And it was given unto him to make war with the saints, and to overcome them:

and there was given to him authority over every tribe and people and tongue and nation."

Comment: The beast makes war against the saints and overcomes them. This includes all saints around the world. The power of the beast has the support of the whole world.

Revelation 13:8-10 "And all that dwell on the earth shall worship him, every one whose name hath not been written from the foundation of the world in the book of life of the Lamb that hath been slain. If any man hath an ear, let him hear. If any man is for captivity, into captivity he goeth: if any man shall kill with the sword, with the sword must he be killed. Here is the patience and the faith of the saints."

Comment: The saints round the world come under the power of the beast, but refuse to worship the beast. Some countries do not believe in capital punishment, and will put the saints in prison, but others do and they will kill them.

Daniel 7:23-25 "Thus he said, The fourth beast shall be a fourth kingdom upon earth, which shall be diverse from all the kingdoms, and shall devour the whole earth, and shall tread it down, and break it in pieces. And as for the ten horns, out of this kingdom shall ten kings arise: and another shall arise after them; and he shall be diverse from the former, and he shall put down three kings."

Comment: The little horn comes up among the ten horns and three horns are removed. Thus the picture of the dragon in Revelation, Chapter 12 is completed for mankind to understand (seven heads, ten horns, and seven diadems). This little horn will probably be the dragon's representative, who helps bring the world against Israel. He will be the representative of the image of the beast set up in the temple which mankind is forced to worship as god. **Matthew 24:15** "When therefore ye see the abomination of desolation, which was spoken of through Daniel the prophet, standing in the holy place (let him that readeth understand)." **II Thessalonians 2:3** "let no man beguile you in any wise: for *it will not be,* except the falling away come first, and the man of sin be revealed, the son of perdition."

The False Prophet

> *Revelation 13:11-13 "And I saw another beast coming up <u>out of the earth</u>; and he had two horns like unto lamb, and he spake as a dragon. And he exerciseth all the authority of the first beast in his sight. And <u>he maketh</u> the earth and them dwell therein <u>to worship</u> the <u>first beast</u>, whose death-stroke was healed. And he doeth great signs, that he should even make <u>fire to come down</u> out of heaven upon the earth in the sight of men."*

Comment: The false prophet comes out of the earth, signifying an appointed kingdom, not one elected from mankind. He has authority just like the first beast. Thus he is either the clay or the iron of the feet in Nebuchadnezzar's image. The false prophet causes mankind to worship the first beast. He does this through supernatural signs such as causing lightning to come down out of the sky.

> *Revelation 13:14-15 "And he <u>deceiveth</u> them that dwell on the earth by reason of the signs which it was given him to do in the sight of the beast; saying to them that dwell on the earth, that they should make an image to the <u>beast who hath the stroke of the sword</u> <u>and lived</u>. And it was given unto him to give breath to it, even to the image of the beast, that the image of the beast should both speak, and cause that as many as should <u>not worship</u> the image of the beast <u>should be killed</u>."*

<u>Comment:</u> He convinces mankind by deception to worship the first beast. He deceives mankind into making an image of the beast, which they can worship. This image represents the head that had victory over the mortal wound. Satan allows the false prophet to give breath to the image, making it possible for this image to speak and convincing the world to kill those who do not worship the image.

> *Revelation 13:16-17 "And he causeth all, the small and the great, and the rich and the poor, and the free and the bond, that there be given them a mark on their right hand, or upon their forehead; and that <u>no man should be able to buy or to sell</u>, save he that hath the mark, even the name of the beast or the number of his name."*

Comment: Complete control over all mankind is accomplished when mankind is unable to buy or sell without joining his system. Each person must receive a mark identifying him and showing that he has joined the system. Today we can understand how a microchip under the skin would accomplish this. There would be no stolen identity, they could locate each person by global satellite positioning, and they could control crime, the world financial system, health records, and so forth. Through the promise of personal security they would be able to control every aspect of our lives.

> *Revelation 13:18 "Here is wisdom. He that hath understanding, let him count the number of the beast; for it is <u>the number of a man</u>: and <u>his number</u> is Six hundred and sixty and six."*

Comment: This system will be able to identify each person by a number. The false prophet's number is 666, which will identify who he is.

The vision Daniel saw which seems to shed light on the false prophet is found in Daniel, Chapter 8.

> *Daniel 8:25 "And through his policy he shall <u>cause craft to prosper</u> in his hand; and he shall magnify himself in his heart, and in <u>their security</u> shall he destroy many: he shall also <u>stand up against the prince of princes</u>; but he shall be <u>broken without hand</u>."*

Comment: The connecting link between Revelation and Daniel's evil king is deception. He also is broken without hand when he stands up against Christ, thus he would be either the false prophet or the beast. He destroys many by giving them the hope of security.

Daniel 8:23 *"And in the latter time of their kingdom, when the transgressors are come to the full, a* <u>*king of fierce countenance,*</u> *and* <u>*understanding dark sentences,*</u> *shall stand up. "*

<u>**Comment:**</u> This king is referred to in the singular form, thus he is not the beast with ten horns. Daniel's vision in Chapter 8 traces the background of the false prophet, indicating he will arise out of the area where the four horns came out of the empire of Greece. He would also represent the iron of Nebuchadnezzar's image (the Roman Empire). The Pope is chosen from countries around the world; thus I believe the False Prophet will come from the area of the world represented by the four horns.

Summary of The Dragon, The Ten -Horned Beast and The False Prophet

Satan himself spearheads the evil forces that are determined to blaspheme God and destroy His people. He accomplishes his desires through the beast and the false prophet. Satan does not physically manifest himself to mankind, yet he has a representative who is one of the three who bring the world against Israel. All three of these representatives are demon-possessed. My conviction is that Satan's message is delivered to mankind and he receives their worship through the image placed in the temple. The ten-horned beast and the false prophet form the eighth and final world kingdom ruling over Israel before Christ's return. This kingdom comes from the same area of the world as the previous seven heads. Satan is able to subject mankind with physical force through the ten-horned beast. The beast has power from Satan to overcome the followers of God, even the final two witnesses. Satan's deception of mankind is accomplished through the false prophet. The false prophet deceives mankind into making an image where Satan can receive their worship. This image also has the ability to speak, delivering Satan's message of "Either worship the image or be killed." He also causes the world to create a system of financial control, so that mankind will not be able to buy or sell without being a part of this system. For this system to be enforced he must have representatives around the world. I believe Satan's personal representative is the little horn, before which three horns of the beast are plucked up. He controls the worship of the image and the destruction of those who do not worship it.

****

God's Message to Mankind in the Book of Revelation

God's messages to mankind are found in Revelation, Chapter 14. There we find three angels with different messages. Their messages to mankind are delivered one after the other. At the end of Revelation, John is told not to seal up the book because it begins now. **Revelation 22:10** "And he saith unto me, Seal not up the words of the prophecy of this book; for the time is at hand." With the fall of Babylon, we discover the first angel has already delivered his message.

First Angel:

Revelation 14:6-7 "And I saw another angel flying in mid heaven, having eternal good tidings to proclaim unto them that dwell on the earth, and unto every nation and tribe and tongue and people; and he saith with a great voice, Fear God, and give him glory; for the hour of <u>his judgment is come</u>: and worship him that made the heaven and the earth and sea and fountains of waters."

<u>**Comment:**</u> Assuming we are presently arriving at the completion of the fall of Babylon, we realize that the first angel's message was delivered by Jesus in **John 12:31-32** "Now is the judgment of this world: now shall the prince of this world be cast out. And I, if I be lifted up from the earth, will draw all men unto myself." This message continued to be delivered down through the Church Age by the followers of Christ.

Revelation 14:1-5 "And I saw, and behold, the Lamb standing on the <u>mount Zion</u>, and <u>with him a hundred and forty and four thousand</u>, having his name, and the name of his Father, written on their foreheads. And I heard a voice from heaven, as the voice of many waters, and as the voice of a great thunder: and the voice which I heard was as the voice of harpers harping with their harps: and they sing as it were a new song before the throne, and before the four living creatures and the elders: and no man could learn the song save the

hundred and forty and four thousand, **even** *they that had been purchased out of the earth. These are they that were not defiled with women; for they are virgins. These* **are** *they that follow the Lamb whithersoever he goeth. These were purchased from among men,* **to be** *the firstfruits unto God and unto the Lamb. And in their mouth was found no lie: they are without blemish."*

<u>**Comment:**</u> God announces during the first angel's message that there are one hundred and forty-four thousand that are purchased from among men as first fruits. In Bible the first fruits are what was sacrificed on the altar. These are those that experience martyrdom during the Church Age, and only they can sing of this experience from their sacrifice. Mount Zion is were Jesus was crucified.

Second Angel:

Revelation 14:8 "And another, a second angel, followed, saying, <u>*Fallen, fallen is*</u> <u>*Babylon*</u> *the great, that hath made all the nations to drink of the wine of the wrath of her fornication."*

<u>**Comment:**</u> The second angel's message of Babylon's fall will be delivered to mankind in the same manner, which is by God's followers. They realize that the prophecy has been fulfilled. The emphasis changes from that of the first message. This doesn't negate the first angel's message, but adds new revelation.

Third Angel:

Revelation 14:9-12 "And another angel, a third, followed them, saying with a great voice, <u>If any man worshippeth the beast and his image, and receiveth a mark on his forehead, or upon his hand, he also shall drink of the wine of the wrath of God</u>, which is prepared unmixed in the cup of his anger; and he shall be tormented with fire and brimstone in the presence of the holy angels, and in the presence of the Lamb: and the smoke of their torment goeth up for ever and ever; and they have no rest day and night, they that worship the beast and his image, and whoso receiveth the mark of his name. Here is the patience of the saints, they that keep the commandments of God, and the faith of Jesus."

<u>Comment:</u> The third angel's message also will be delivered by God's followers. The emphasis will be, "Don't worship the beast by taking his mark." During this time God once again is defending Israel. The delivery of this message to mankind begins with the 144,000 Jews that are sealed (12,000 from each tribe). The final message to mankind from God during the tribulation will be delivered by the two witnesses in Chapter 11. They have power the power to smite the earth with every plague as often as they desire. Their deaths are celebrated by mankind, because the world thinks they have stopped the plagues of God's wrath which the two witnesses were delivering.

Matthew 24:14 "And this gospel of the kingdom shall be <u>preached in the whole world</u> for a

testimony unto all the nations; and then shall the end come."

Comment: Here we are told God's message will be preached in the entire world for a testimony, and then the end will come. Just as the whole world sees the bodies of the two witnesses lying dead in the streets, they will have heard God's message through them.

Revelation 14:14-20 "And I saw, and behold, a white cloud; and on the cloud I saw one sitting like unto a son of man, having on his head a golden crown, and in his hand a sharp sickle. And another angel came out from the temple, crying with a great voice to him that sat on the cloud, Send forth thy sickle, and reap: for the hour to reap is come; for the <u>harvest of the earth is ripe</u>. And he that sat on the cloud cast his sickle upon the earth; and the earth was reaped. Another angel came out from the temple which is in heaven, he also having a sharp sickle. And another angel came out from the altar, he that hath power over fire; and he called with a great voice to him that had the sharp sickle, saying, Send forth thy sharp sickle, and gather the clusters of the vine of the earth; for her grapes are fully ripe. And the angel cast his sickle into the earth, and gathered the vintage of the earth, and cast it into the winepress, <u>the great winepress</u>, of the wrath of God. And the winepress are trodden without the city, and there came out blood from the winepress, even <u>unto</u>

the bridles of the horses, as far as a thousand and six hundred furlongs."

Matthew 24:38-42 "For as in those days which were before the flood they were eating and drinking, marrying and giving in marriage, until the day that Noah entered into the ark, and they knew not until the flood came, and took them all away; so shall be the coming of the Son of man. Then shall two men be in the field; <u>one is taken</u>, and one is left: two women **shall** *be grinding at the mill; one is taken, and <u>one is left</u>. Watch therefore: for ye know not on what day your Lord cometh."*

Matthew 13:40-42 "As therefore <u>the tares are gathered up and burned with fire</u>; so shall it be in the end of the world. The Son of man shall send forth <u>his angels</u>, and they shall gather out of his kingdom all things that cause stumbling, and them that do iniquity, and shall cast them into the furnace of fire: there shall be the weeping and the gnashing of teeth."

Comment: The end brings the gathering of the tares by the angels, and casting them into the lake of fire. Those people who endure to the end will be gathered into God's Kingdom.

Revelation 22:17 "And the Spirit and <u>the bride say, Come</u>. And he that heareth, let him say, Come. And he that is athirst, let him come: he that will, let him take the water of life freely."

Comment: Here we find further evidence that God's followers will deliver His message to mankind. The Holy Spirit transforms the believers during the Church Age; they are the Bride of Christ. They in turn testify to those they come in contact with, inviting them to be part of God's Kingdom.

Believers During the Tribulation

> *Revelation 7:16 "They <u>shall hunger</u> no more, <u>neither thirst</u> any more; neither shall the sun strike <u>upon them sun strike, nor any heat.</u>"*

Comment: They experience hunger, thirst, and the sun scorching them. Not only do they go through the plagues of the tribulation, but also the privileges of a normal life are denied them because they refuse to join the world system.

> *Revelation 13:7-8 "And it was given unto him to make <u>war with the saints</u>, and to <u>overcome them:</u> and there was given to him <u>authority over every tribe and people and tongue and nation.</u> And all that dwell on the earth shall worship him, every one whose name hath not been written from the foundation of the world in the book of life of the Lamb that hath been slain."*

Comment: The beast uses his power to make war with the saints in every part of the world. The saints are overcome by the forces of the beast,. The whole world worships the beast. Only the saints will have the knowledge and the willpower to refuse.

Revelation 13:10 "If any man is for <u>captivity</u>, into captivity he goeth: if any man shall <u>kill</u> with the sword, with the sword must he be killed. Here is the patience and the faith of the saints."

<u>Comment</u>: The message of the saints will be silenced. Those countries that believe in capital punishment will kill the saints. The other countries will put them in captivity. This experience will try the patience of the saints, since by simply joining the world system and worshiping Satan, they could be freed.

Revelation 14:12 "Here is the <u>patience of the saints</u>, they that keep the commandments of God, and the faith of Jesus."

<u>Comment</u>: The patience of the saints will be tried as they keep God's commandments. They realize the torment coming to them from the followers of the beast can in no way compare to God's blessing to those who are faithful to Him. They will be willing to give up their lives before worshiping Satan.

Revelation 14:13 "And I heard the voice from heaven saying, Write, <u>Blessed are the</u> <u>dead who die in the Lord</u> from henceforth: yea, saith the Spirit, that they may rest from their labors; for their works follow with them."

<u>Comment</u>: When the saints are killed, they enter into God's blessing.

Revelation 12:17 "And the dragon waxed <u>wroth</u> <u>with the woman</u>, and went away to make <u>war</u> <u>with the rest of her seed</u>, that keep the commandments of God, and hold the testimony of Jesus:"

<u>Comment:</u> They experience Satan's wrath as he seeks to destroy completely those who follow Jesus.

Revelation 12:11 "And they overcame him because of the <u>blood of the Lamb</u>, and because of the word of their <u>testimony</u>; and they loved not their life even unto death."

<u>Comment:</u> The saints overcome Satan the same way all believers have, through the shed blood of Jesus and with their testimony of that to the world. The believers during the tribulation will be the ones who announce to mankind that by receiving the mark of the beast they will be condemned to hell for their rejection of Jesus. They overcome Satan by their testimony.

Matthew 24:13 "But he that <u>endureth</u> to the end, the same shall be saved."

<u>Comment:</u> The followers of God during the tribulation are told to endure to the end in order to be to be saved. They must not give in to the lawlessness and pressures that are against them on all sides. They also must endure the darkness that follows the tribulation. From the number of days mentioned in **Daniel 12:11-12** "And from the time that the

continual *burnt-offering* shall be taken away, and the abomination that maketh desolate set up, there shall be a thousand and two hundred and ninety days. Blessed is he that waiteth, and cometh to the thousand three hundred and five and thirty day," it would appear there will be 45 days of waiting.

After the Battle of Armageddon

> *Matthew 24:29-30 "But immediately after the tribulation of those days the <u>sun shall be darkened, and the moon shall not give her light</u>, and the stars shall fall from heaven, and the powers of the heavens shall be shaken: and then shall appear the sign of the Son of man in heaven: and then shall all the tribes of the earth mourn, and they shall see the Son of man coming on the clouds of heaven with power and great glory."*

<u>Comment:</u> We are told that with the end of the tribulation and before Christ's return, the sun will be darkened and the powers of the heavens shaken. The earth will no longer be in the orbit around the sun that it is today. Remaining mankind sit in darkness until they see Christ's return with great glory.

> *Matthew 24:27 "For as the <u>lightning cometh</u> forth from the east, and is seen even unto the west; so shall be the coming of the Son of man."*

Comment: Christ's return will be like the lightning lighting up the sky. This will be how mankind is to recognize the true Christ.

> *Matthew 24:24-26 "For there shall arise false Christs, and false prophets, and shall show great signs and wonders; so as to lead astray, if possible, <u>even the elect</u>. Behold, I have told you beforehand. If therefore they shall say unto you, Behold, he is in the wilderness; go not forth: Behold, he is in the inner chambers; believe it not."*

Comment: We are warned not to follow any other religion or person that does not meet the description of the lightning. Jesus gave this warning because He knows deception will be great, even to the point of deceiving the elect.

> *Luke 1:78 -79 "Because of the tender mercy of our God, Whereby the dayspring from on high shall visit us, To shine upon them that sit in darkness and the shadow of death; To <u>guide our feet into the way of peace</u>."*

Comment: Mankind will sit in darkness, hopelessly expecting death. Jesus' return will give light to guide their feet into life and the way to peace.

> *Isaiah 60:1-5 "Arise, shine; for thy light is come, and the glory of Jehovah is risen upon thee. For, behold, darkness shall cover the earth, and gross darkness the peoples; but Jehovah will arise*

*upon thee, and <u>his glory shall be seen upon thee</u>.
And nations shall <u>come to thy light</u>, and kings to
the <u>brightness of thy rising</u>. <u>Lift up thine eyes
round about, and see</u>: they all gather themselves
together, they come to thee; thy sons shall come
from far, and thy daughters shall be carried in
the arms. Then thou shalt see and <u>be radiant</u>,
and thy heart shall thrill and be enlarged;
because the abundance of the sea shall be turned
unto thee, the <u>wealth of the nations shall come
unto thee</u>."*

Comment: Isaiah reveals more details of Christ's return.
Mankind finds them-selves in gross darkness when suddenly
there is a change. The faces of God's people become radiant,
lighting up their surroundings. We have an example of a face
glowing in the scriptures, that of Moses after being in God's
presence. The nations will move toward those with light. They
will bring their wealth and will desire to be a part of the light
God gives to His elect.

*Isaiah 60:19-21 "The sun shall be no more thy
light by day; neither for brightness shall the
moon give light unto thee: but <u>Jehovah</u> will be
unto thee an <u>everlasting light</u>, and thy God thy
glory. Thy sun shall no more go down, neither
shall thy moon withdraw itself; for Jehovah will
be thine everlasting light, and the days of thy
mourning shall be ended. Thy people also shall
be all righteous; they shall inherit the land for
ever, the branch of my planting, the work of my
hands, that I may be glorified."*

Comment: The sun and moon no longer will be the source of light. God will be an everlasting light. The Scriptures tell us with God there is no darkness at all.

> *Matthew 13:43 "Then shall the righteous shine forth as the <u>sun in the kingdom</u> of their Father. He that hath ears, let him hear."*

Comment: The righteous people that enter the Kingdom when Jesus returns will shine like the sun does today.

> *Matthew 24:31 "And he shall send forth his angels with a great sound of a trumpet, and they <u>shall gather together his elect</u> from the four winds, <u>from</u> one <u>end of heaven</u> to the other."*

Comment: The angels bring together God's elect. This includes the resurrection of those killed during the tribulation.

> *Zechariah 14:6-7 "And it shall come to pass in that day, that there shall not be light; the bright ones shall withdraw themselves: but it shall be <u>one day</u> which is known unto Jehovah; <u>not day, and not night</u>; but it shall come to pass, that at evening time there shall be light."*

Comment: There will be only light time in Christ's kingdom. Daytime will be continuous.

II Peter 3:8 "But forget not this one thing, beloved, that one day is with the Lord as a thousand years, and a <u>thousand years as one day</u>."

Comment: When Christ rules and reigns for 1,000 years on earth, there will be no night, just one day. To God, one day is the same as 1,000 years are to us.

Zechariah 8:23 "Thus saith Jehovah of hosts: In those days* it shall come to pass, *that ten men shall take hold, out of all the languages of the nations, they shall take hold of the <u>skirt of him that is a Jew</u>, saying, We will <u>go with you</u>, for we have heard that God is with you."

Comment: The nations will beg to go up with a Jew to worship God in Jerusalem. To me it seems when God's people go to Jerusalem to worship God and when they are in His presence, it will make their faces shine. You might say they get their batteries recharged. When they return home, they light up their neighborhoods. This also gives their crops the energy needed to grow.

Daniel 12:3 "And they that are <u>wise shall shine</u> as the brightness of the firmament; and they that turn many to righteousness as the stars for ever and ever."

Comment: God's followers will reflect His light. They will light up His universe forever. God has plans to show off His followers. It is possible that those in outer darkness will be able to see what is in the light. The rich man in **Luke 16:23**

was able to see Lazarus in Abraham's bosom. There is no mention of Lazarus being able to see the rich man. The great gulf between them could be explained by trying to mix light and darkness.

Conclusion

The Scriptures make it clear that there are two sides to life: the dark side and the light side. Mankind is given the opportunity to choose during this life. Will the person choose God and seek to follow his instructions, or will he reject God's provision of salvation through Jesus Christ? By blaspheming God's name, joining the side of Satan and self-satisfaction, he becomes his own god. The final result will be as different as eternal light (life) is from eternal darkness (death). The results will last forever. Jesus Christ is the victor and will punish all evil. Every knee will bow to him. **I. Timothy 5:24-25** "Some men's sins are evident, going before unto judgment; and some men also they follow after. In like manner also there are good works that are evident; and such as are otherwise cannot be hid." Every individual's life will be exposed. Today is the day of salvation and Jesus stands at the door knocking. Have you invited Him into your life or will your life be one of rejecting Him? The days of this life are short and the offer of God's gift of salvation does not extend beyond it.

Satan Creates his Image on Earth

Revelation 17:8 $\longrightarrow$ *was* —————

Daniel 2:31-45	Rev. 13: 1 Seven heads (Blaspheme God by placing their gods over Isreal)	Rev 17:10 (When John wrote Rev.)
Nebuchadnezzar's Image	❶ Eygpt $\longrightarrow$	
	❷ Assyria $\longrightarrow$	
Head - Gold $\longrightarrow$	❸ Babylon $\longrightarrow$	Five are fallen
Breast+Arms - Silver $\rightarrow$	❹ MedoPersia $\longrightarrow$	
Belly+Thighs - Brass $\rightarrow$	❺ Greece $\longrightarrow$	
Legs - Iron $\longrightarrow$	❻ Rome $\longrightarrow$	one is
Feet - Iron Clay $\longrightarrow$	❼ Islamic Empire $\longrightarrow$	yet to come

Satan Creates his Image on Earth *(Continued)*

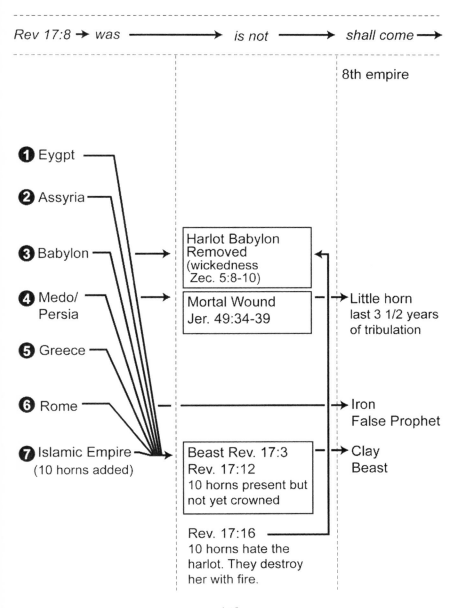

Rev 17:8 → was ────────→ is not ────────→ shall come →

8th empire

❶ Eygpt

❷ Assyria

❸ Babylon → Harlot Babylon Removed (wickedness Zec. 5:8-10)

❹ Medo/ Persia → Mortal Wound Jer. 49:34-39 —— → Little horn last 3 1/2 years of tribulation

❺ Greece

❻ Rome —— → Iron False Prophet

❼ Islamic Empire (10 horns added) → Beast Rev. 17:3 Rev. 17:12 10 horns present but not yet crowned —— → Clay Beast

Rev. 17:16 10 horns hate the harlot. They destroy her with fire.

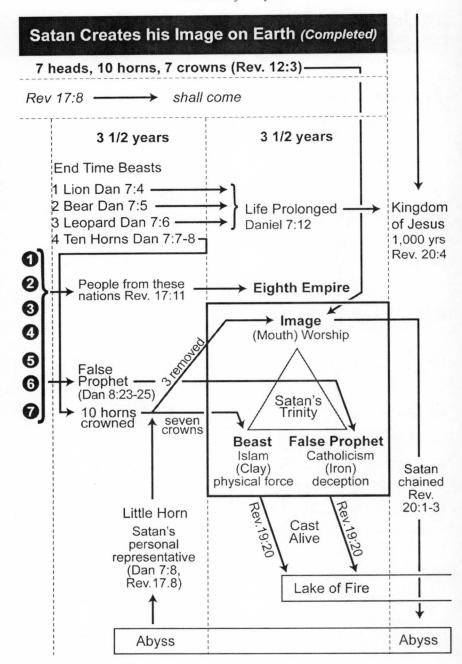

Advantage Books
PO Box 160847
Altamonte Springs, FL 32716

info@advbooks.com

To purchase additional copies of this book or other books published by Advantage
Books call our toll free order number at:
1-888-383-3110 (Book Orders Only)

or visit our bookstore website at:
www.advbookstore.com

Longwood, Florida, USA
"we bring dreams to life"™
www.advbooks.com

LaVergne, TN USA
24 August 2010
194472LV00003B/22/P